Disclaimer Notice:

Please note the information contained within this document is for educational and entertainment purposes only. All effort has been executed to present accurate, up to date, reliable, complete information. No warranties of any kind are declared or implied. Readers acknowledge that the author is not engaged in the rendering of legal, financial, medical, or professional advice. The content within this book has been derived from various sources. Please consult a licensed professional before attempting any techniques outlined in this book.

CONTENTS

Introduction

Ice cream: A yummy dessert that is fun for everyone! (This delicious dessert came from an earlier iced cream or cream ice) is a sweetened frozen food typically eaten as a snack or dessert. It is usually made from dairy products, such as milk and cream, and often combined with fruits or other ingredients and flavors.

BEST ICE CREAM YOU'LL EVER MAKE!

Some of the best ice cream you will ever eat will be made right in your very own kitchen! That's right...this book will show you how to become a master at your craft as an "Ice Cream Scoopologist!" ⍰ You will be surprised at how simple-n-easy this book and its recipes are to use. I'm sure you will be impressed once your friends love you for the thought of making something nice, sweet and creamy to eat. Let's be real about one thing...That is, EVERYONE LOVES ICE CREAM! Kids and adults alike, fantasize about all of the available flavors that run through your mind when just thinking about this delicious dessert.

MAKE YOUR OWN CHOICES!

The great thing about making your very own ice cream is that you can control exactly what is in it. Everyone now days at least makes an effort to eat as healthy as possible. There are many ways for you to make ice cream in a healthier way that you get it at the store. Substitutions are the key. We show you how to substitute ingredients to make a healthier ice cream for you, your friends and family. The choice is up to you and options are endless!

Now ...invite that special someone of yours over and start scooping that ice cream ;)

Ice Cream Accessories, Yes...A Must!
The Foundation for Something Delicious! ;)

Just eating ice cream alone is already a very delicious thing, indeed! However, nothing beats a double chocolate mint scoop of ice cream in a waffle cone. What about a waffle cone with sprinkles around the rim. Or, a sugar dipped waffle bowl with your favorite candy bar to add to it. There is such a variety of delicious avenues to serve your new homemade dessert. You better make sure to get creative with these recipes! Now this is the section where all the fun begins!

THIS IS JUST AN IDEA OF HOW CREATIVE YOU CAN BE. COME UP WITH A LIST OF FAVORITES!

- Waffle cone or cup
- Sugar cone
- Pretzel cone
- On pancakes or crepes
- On waffles
- On pie
- On cake
- On donuts
- On brownies
- In cookie cups
- In a chocolate-dipped tortilla
- In between two cookies
- In a pie crust bowl
- In a cream puff
- On top of a grilled peach
- In between 2 pieces of pound cake

Why Add Toppings???

I think it would be a pretty boring world without the "mastery...creativeness and swagger" in art of making the perfect scoop! This is where you can really go wild and have some fun. There's literally endless possibilities here. Any snack you enjoy will probably go with some type of ice cream. Fresh fruit is always a good healthy choice. Here are some choices to spark your imagination. Let us know what you come up with!

List of Possible Toppings:

- Apples
- Apricots
- Avocado
- Bananas
- Blackberries
- Blueberries
- Breakfast Cereal
- Brownies
- Candy
- Candy Bars (Chopped)
- Cantaloupe
- Cherries
- Chex Mix
- Chocolate Chips
- Chocolate Covered Pretzels
- Cinnamon
- Clementine
- Cocoa Powder
- Coconut
- Cookies
- Cranberries
- Crushed Lollipops
- Currants
- Dates
- Dried Fruit
- Figs
- Graham Crackers
- Grapefruit
- Grapes
- Guava
- Gummy Bears
- Honeydew Melon
- Jackfruit
- Jelly Beans
- Kiwi
- Kumquat
- Lemons
- Limes
- Mandarin
- Mango
- Marshmallows
- Melon
- Mochi
- Mulberries
- Nectarine
- Nutmeg
- Nuts
- Olives
- Oranges
- Papaya
- Passion Fruit
- Peaches
- Pears
- Persimmon
- Pineapple
- Plantain
- Plums
- Pomegranate
- Popcorn
- Pretzel Sticks
- Pretzels
- Pummelo
- Pumpkin Spice
- Raisins
- Raspberries
- Rice Cakes
- Sesame Seeds
- Sprinkles
- Strawberries
- Trail Mix
- Vanilla
- Watermelon
- Whipped Cream
- And Much More...

Let's Get <u>Saucy</u>...Be a Sauce Artist!

Sauces add lovely texture and flavor all at once. Sauce doesn't have to go on top however. Use sauces to decorate the plate or bowl. You can make your own sauces and put them in squeeze bottles to create beautiful designs. If you don't have time to make your own, your local grocery store carries many. Here are some sauces that compliment ice cream.

- Chocolate
- White chocolate
- Vanilla
- Butterscotch
- Caramel
- Blueberry
- Strawberry
- Raspberry

- Lemon
- Cherry
- Mocha
- Peanut butter
- Coffee
- Maple syrup
- Praline sauce
- Mint

Pro Tips for Making Great Homemade Ice Cream!

1: Always Remember That a Minimum of 24 Hours is Needed to Freeze Your (Ice Cream Maker Bowl) or Freezing Container Properly. The more it freezes, the harder the bowl will get and this will ensure that your bowl will stay cold throughout the ice cream making process!

2: Do Not Over Fill Your Ice Cream Maker!
1/2 to 2/3 full is where you need to be! When making ice cream of any kind, during the process the ice cream will expand. So, if you overfill the bowl, then you will have "AN ICE CREAM MESS!" If the freezer bowl is not frozen solid for the correct period of time, and the bowl has more ice cream to churn than its coldness can handle, then it will not be long into the ice cream process before it is no longer cold. Remember...you want delicious ice cream! Not Soup!! Lol

3: More Cream = Better Ice Cream.
You can ease up on the milk and add more cream if you would like. You may find that this is the most delicious tip you've ever heard about this wonderful dessert! If you think about it...the cream is also sweet and adds a richness to each and every tasty mouthful!

4: Use a Blender or Food Processer for Sugars and Fresh Spices.
You will find that by doing this little trick that your ice cream has a less grainy consistency, making your ice cream silky smooth on the tongue and so delicious to indulge.

5: Add items to your ice cream that have a creamy consistency.
If you add items that will give a creamy consistency to your ice cream then you will be in heaven when you realize how much "deliciousness" you have created! It's yummy, and it's creamy, and it's succulent, and it's Ohhh, sooo good!" You can use any type of items like an avocado, an egg yolks or even yogurt for that matter!

6: Make Sure You Don't Churn on the Hot Stove!
Your ice cream maker makes your ice cream at a very cold temperature. If you attempt to make your ice cream in any environment besides a cool environment, you may end up eating soup or a melted milk shake at best! Remember, you want to get the most freeze out of your bowl. I tell you, if I could, I would make my ice cream in the freezer! lol 🙂

7: Consider Chilling the Ingredients to Keep the Ice Cream Colder...Longer
OK...we already know that the ice cream is going to be very cold. However, during the process you can get an area on the counter that may get warm, or the temperature in the house warms up, etc. by having all of the ingredients chilled will give you the longest chill you can get! It may not seem like much, but a little chill bit of chill can go a long way!

Be the Life of the Party!
Boring Ice Cream Is Now a Thing of the Past!!

What dessert has been craved by kids and adults for all of eternity? That may be an over-exaggeration, but it's ice cream! The frozen treat has delighted so many for so long and now you have the ability to make delicious creations with the Cuisinart Ice-21 1.5 Quart or the Pure Indulgence 2 Quart Frozen Yogurt-Sorbet & Ice Cream Maker by Cuisinart!

Our Treat to You, Ice Cream Cookies!

We're giving you so much to enjoy! There's nothing that goes better with ice cream than smashed between two sweet, desirable, chocolate chipped cookie dough ice cream sandwiches. Sounds more like dessert to most, but sometimes is dinner to me! Lol! I had to laugh at that one but, when you want something tempting and you've been on that meal plan for most of the week...you just need to unwind and take care of yourself. Well, these ice cream cookies will do the job then! All you will ever need! You have varieties to choose from!

Succulent Waffle Cookie Ice Cream Sandwich

Works best with a Mini Waffle, Waffle Maker. Really gets the job done and is small enough to be the perfect size to make ice cream sandwiches.

Preparation Time About: 5 Minutes | **Servings:** 6

INGREDIENTS
1 cup flour
1 tbsp. sugar
2 tsp. baking powder
½ tsp. cinnamon
¼ tsp. salt
1 egg
1 cup milk
1 ½ tbs. melted butter

DIRECTIONS
- Crack eggs and mix in a bowl with salt and pepper.
- Pour 2 tbsps. Milk to the eggs and whisk. Mix in the other ingredients until the batter is smooth.
- Spray your waffle maker with oil. Pour 2 tbsp. batter into the waffle maker and cook until crispy. Repeat until all the batter is used.
- Put a scoop of ice cream (that you made from this book) in the middle of two waffles.
- Drizzle honey over the top for a sweeter experience.

Applesauce Waffle Cookie Ice Cream Sandwich

Works best with a Mini Waffle, Waffle Maker. Really gets the job done and is small enough to be the perfect size to make ice cream sandwiches.

Preparation Time About: 5 Minutes | **Servings:** 6

INGREDIENTS

Simple Applesauce
3 pounds apples combination of McIntosh, Golden Delicious, Granny Smith, Fuji, and Jonathan
1 cup water
2 tablespoons lemon juice
1 3-inch cinnamon stick

Add-Ons (As an option)
1/2 cup brown sugar
2 tablespoons butter
1/2 teaspoon ground cinnamon
1/2 teaspoon vanilla extract

DIRECTIONS

Simple Applesauce Directions
- Cut up apples into small pieces, but peel and core it first. Move the apples to a large pot.
- Add in lemon juice, a stick of cinnamon and water, when it starts to boil over high heat reduce the heat to low and cover to let simmer. About 20-30 min. The apples should be soft.
- Use a blender to puree the applesauce., You can also use a food processor, or immersion blender for a smoother applesauce.

Add-ons: (Optional
- Stir in brown sugar. Cook uncovered till the applesauce thickens up a little bit. about 5-10 minutes. **(Sweeter option)**
- Mix the butter, until butter is melted, with the ground cinnamon, and vanilla extract, Yummy!

Blueberry Pumpkin Spice Waffle Ice Cream Sandwich

Blueberries just make the world go round! A superfood dessert indeed! Blueberries are classified as being a low glycemic food as well. This one is always a good treat! ⬚ .

Preparation Time About: 5 Minutes | **Servings:** 6

INGREDIENTS
1 cup flour
1 tbsp. sugar
2 tsp. baking powder
½ tsp. cinnamon
½ tsp. pumpkin spice
1 cup blueberries (organic)
¼ tsp. salt
1 egg
1 cup milk
1 ½ tbs. melted butter

DIRECTIONS
- Crack eggs and mix in a bowl with salt and pepper.
- Pour 2 tbsps. Milk to the eggs and whisk. Mix in the other ingredients until the batter is smooth.
- Spray your waffle maker with oil. Pour 2 tbsp. batter into the waffle maker and cook until crispy. Repeat until all the batter is used.
- Put a scoop of ice cream (that you made from this book) in the middle of two waffles.
- Drizzle honey over the top for a sweeter experience.

S'mores Ice Cream Dream Cookie Delight

Well, this is a treat! Always remember the days of the camp fires in the back yard and putting marshmallows on a stick getting them nice and toasty. Then scooping your favorite ice cream on one of the graham crackers along with the toasted marshmallows... Yummmmm!

Preparation Time About: 35 Minutes | **Servings:** 6

INGREDIENTS

1 graham cracker
1 scoop ice cream (of your choice)
1/4 c. toasted mini marshmallows
Chocolate sauce, for drizzling

DIRECTIONS

- Get a box if Graham Crackers and break them into squares.
- Then scoop ice cream onto one square and top with toasted marshmallows.
- With the chocolate sauce just drizzle on top. (should be a little messy!)

Candy Cane Ice Cream Sandwiches

This all-time classic combines the delicious flavors of vanilla ice cream and chocolate sandwich cookies. The rich taste of the sandwich cookies is complimented by the subtle creaminess of the vanilla ice cream.

Preparation Time About: 35 Minutes | **Servings:** 6

INGREDIENTS

1 lb. Sugar cookie dough
vanilla ice cream
Crushed candy canes
Sprinkle of cinnamon

DIRECTIONS

- First, make sure you preheat oven to 345 degrees F. Take the sugar cookie dough and make them into 1 tablespoon balls and place them on the parchment baking sheet paper. Put them in the oven and bake till lightly golden brown
- Approximately 10 minutes.
- Let the cookies cool for about 5 minutes on baking sheets
- You can then move them to wire rack to cool.
- Once cool, place giant scoop of ice cream onto one cookie and sandwich with another cookie on top. Roll in lightly crushed candy canes and freeze for about 30min.

Snicker Doodle Ice Cream Sandwiches

This I think is on the top of the charts of the ice cream sandwiches. We love this one recipe! There is just something about the Snicker Doodle! Enjoy!

Preparation Time About: 1 Hours, 15min | **Servings:** 24

INGREDIENTS

1 1/2 cups all-purpose flour
1 teaspoon baking soda
1 teaspoon cream of tartar
1 cup sugar, divided
1/2 cup unsalted butter
1/4 teaspoon kosher salt
1 large egg, room temperature
2 1/4 teaspoons ground cinnamon

DIRECTIONS

- Whisk flour, baking soda, and cream of tartar in a medium bowl. For best results, use an electric mixer on medium
- Beat butter in a large bowl, about 2 to 2 1/2 minutes, beating the mix until light and fluffy
- Take the dough, put it into a ball, wrap ball in plastic wrap then chill it for about a 30min.
- Preheat oven to 400°F. Put parchment paper on 2 baking sheets.
- Take the remaining 1/4 cup sugar and cinnamon, in a small bowl and mix it.
- Roll balls in cinnamon sugar using your hands to do so into a tablespoonful of dough balls.
- Transfer dough balls to baking sheet about 1" - 2" apart from each other.
- Bake until golden brown on the edges. About 10 minutes
- Transfer to a wire rack to cook

Blueberry Honey English Muffin Ice Cream Sandwich

Some people just think up anything to put or to go with ice cream. This one is so simple but very enjoyable! Enjoy!

Preparation Time About: 15min | **Servings:** 2

INGREDIENTS
1 pack of English muffins
organic honey to pour atop
small pack of blueberries

DIRECTIONS
- Toast your English muffins in a toaster just like you would for breakfast.
- Spread about 4-5 blueberries on top of your warm muffin.
- Squeeze out and drizzle honey over both inside pieces of the English muffin.
- Add a scoop of Ice Cream (that you made from this book) between the two pieces of English muffins.
- Enjoy!

Honey Cinnamon Blackberry English Muffin Ice Cream Sandwich

Some people just think up anything to put or to go with ice cream. This one is so simple but very enjoyable! Enjoy!

Preparation Time About: 15min | **Servings:** 2

INGREDIENTS
1 pack of English muffins
organic honey to pour atop
small pack of blackberries
1 tsp. cinnamon

DIRECTIONS
- Toast your English muffins in a toaster just like you would for breakfast.
- Spread about 4-5 blackberries on top of your warm muffin.
- Squeeze out and drizzle honey over both inside pieces of the English muffin.
- Sprinkle a little cinnamon on top
- Add a scoop of Ice Cream (that you made from this book) between the two pieces of English muffins. Enjoy!

Strawberry English Muffin with Honey Ice Cream Sandwich

Some people just think up anything to put or to go with ice cream. This one is so simple but very enjoyable! Enjoy!

Preparation Time About: 15min | **Servings:** 2

INGREDIENTS
1 pack of English muffins
organic honey to pour atop
small pack of strawberries
DIRECTIONS
- Toast your English muffins in a toaster just like you would for breakfast.
- Spread about 4-5 strawberries on top of your warm muffin.
- Squeeze out and drizzle honey over both inside pieces of the English muffin.
- Add a scoop of Ice Cream (that you made from this book) between the two pieces of English muffins. Enjoy!

Mango Texas Toast Ice Cream Sandwich

This one is just down right "Delicious"! Straight to the point with no excuses! When you try this one...you'll be hooked for life!

Preparation Time About: 15min | **Servings:** 2

INGREDIENTS
1 loaf of Texas Toast bread (thick slices)
organic honey to pour atop
1 mango (peeled & sliced)
DIRECTIONS
- Toast your Texas Toast in a toaster. It should be nice and firm and golden brown.
- Spread some of the mango slices on top of your Texas Toast.
- Squeeze out and drizzle honey over both inside pieces of the Texas Toast.
- Add a scoop of Ice Cream (that you made from this book) between the two pieces of Texas Toast and Enjoy!

Apple Cinnamon Almond Butter Top Roman Ice Cream Sandwich

Not sure if you've ever heard of this one but, "Don't knock it till you try it!" This dessert will give you that crunch that you are looking for that pairs well with that soft delicious, ice cream feeling!

Preparation Time About: 10min | **Servings:** 2

INGREDIENTS
1 pack top roman noodles (remove season)
1 tsp. cinnamon
1 tablespoon of almond butter
½ apple (peeled, cored, and finely diced)

DIRECTIONS
- Open the pack of top roman. Break it in half so you have 2 slices.
- Spread some of the almond butter on top of both slices of Top Roman.
- Spread the finely diced apples on top of the almond butter (apples warmed is amazing!!!)
- Sprinkle a little bit of cinnamon on the almond butter.
- Add a scoop of Ice Cream (that you made from this book) between the two pieces of Top Roman, almond butter and apples… A real treat indeed! Enjoy!

Chocolate Almond Butter Top Roman Ice Cream Sandwich

This dessert dish will put you in a better mood all the way around. You'll be looking forward to getting home from work for this one. Trust me…it may not last too long in that refrigerator when your family or friends know this one is in there!

Preparation Time About: 10min | **Servings:** 2

INGREDIENTS
1 pack top roman noodles (remove season)
6oz. Hershey's milk chocolate
1 tablespoon of almond butter

DIRECTIONS
- Open the pack of top roman. Break it in half so you have 2 slices.
- Spread some of the almond butter on top of both slices of Top Roman.
- Melt the chocolate in the microwave at ½ power for 1 min. (repeat if necessary).
- Add a scoop of Ice Cream (that you made from this book) between the two pieces of Top Roman, drizzle on some of that melted chocolate… and Enjoy!

Size Conversion Chart for Various Size Makers
Note: The recipes in this book are made from a 1.5qt. and 2qt. container.
***If using a 1.5qt. container DO NOT over fill your bowl! You may have some left overs. for later for making a little more later.**
Follow the chart and main ingredients for the size container you have!
For Adults Only: Remember that over 4 tbsp. of alcohol makes it hard for ice cream to freeze. Use 4 tbsp. on larger qts. then add more alcohol if needed.

ICE CREAM INGREDIENTS	MAKES 2QT.	MAKES 4QT.	MAKES 6QT.
heavy cream	2 cups	4 cups	6 cups
milk	1 cup	2 cups	4 cups
sugar	¾ cup	½ cup	1 ¼ cups
vanilla extract	1 tbsp.	2 tbsp.	3 tbsp.
fruit & other ingredients	same as book	double amount	triple amount
alcohol	3 tbsp. or less	4 tbsp. or less	5 tbsp. or less
MILKSHAKE INGREDIENTS	**MAKES 2QT.**	**MAKES 4QT.**	**MAKES 6QT.**
heavy cream	2 cups	4 cups	6 cups
milk	1 cup	2 cups	4 cups
sugar	¾ cup	½ cup	1 ¼ cups
vanilla extract	1 tbsp.	2 tbsp.	3 tbsp.
fruit & other ingredients	same as book	double amount	triple amount
alcohol	3 tbsp. or less	4 tbsp. or less	5 tbsp. or less
SORBET INGREDIENTS	**MAKES 2QT.**	**MAKES 4QT.**	**MAKES 6QT.**
Each recipe varies. Refer to each ingredient.	Same as book. Ingredients	Dble. Ingredient Alc. 4-5 tbsp.	Tripl. Ingredient Alc. 4-5 tbsp.
GELATO INGREDIENTS	**MAKES 2QT.**	**MAKES 4QT.**	**MAKES 6QT.**
heavy cream	2 cups	4 cups	6 cups
milk	1 cup	2 cups	4 cups
sugar	¾ cup	½ cup	1 ¼ cups
vanilla extract	1 tbsp.	2 tbsp.	3 tbsp.
fruit & other ingredients	same as book	double amount	Triple amount
alcohol	3 tbsp. or less	4 tbsp. or less	5 tbsp. or less
FROZ. YOGURT INGREDIENTS	**MAKES 2QT.**	**MAKES 4QT.**	**MAKES 6QT.**
full-fat plain yogurt	1 qt. container	2 qt. container	4 qt. container
salt	¼ tsp.	½ tsp.	¾ tsp.
sugar	1 cup	2 cups	3 cups
extract (any extract)	1 tsp.	2 tsp.	3 tsp.
fruit & other ingredients	same as book	double amount	triple amount
alcohol	3 tbsp. or less	4 tbsp. or less	5 tbsp. or less

Quick Start Steps – Instructions for Our Recipes
NOTE: Our recipes are made with the Cuisinart 30BC 2qt. and Ice-21 1.5qt. Ice Cream Makers.
These are the steps we've found to be the most useful for these products.

1	**FREEZE YOUR BOWL!** We touched on this earlier, but make sure to freeze the freezer bowl in your freezer for at least 6 hours prior to making ice cream, but no more than 22 hours. After you wash and dry your bowl before freezing it, make sure to wrap it in plastic wrap so it doesn't get freezer burn. Store it in the coldest part of your freezer: the back.

2	Make sure your ice cream maker is clean and ready to use (even wash it before first use). Remember, wipe the base with a damp cloth, and then the freezer bowl, lid, and mixing arm with warm water and dish soap.
3	Prepare the ingredients in the recipes in a separate container beforehand. Make sure you can pour easily from your mixing container.
4	The bowl is designed to make no more than either 1.5 Quarts for the Cuisinart ICE-21 or 2 quarts for the Pure Indulgence, and **make sure not to fill the freezer bowl all the way to the top, leaving at least ½" of room**. The ingredients will increase the volume so be careful!
5	Attach the churning device/mixing arm. Don't be alarmed if the arm is not snug. It is designed to loosely rest in the bowl.
6	Secure the lid firmly.
7	Turn on the ice cream maker. The freezer bowl will then begin to rotate.
8	Pour your ingredients immediately, but slowly, through the top opening in the lid.
9	Let the creaming begin! Wait for 25-35 minutes depending on the recipe and then turn off the ice cream maker and transfer the concoction to another container, placing in the freezer for an additional 2 hours or more. Then enjoy!

Instructions for a General Ice Cream Freezer Bowl

These basic instructions work for any stand mixer ice cream maker bowl that goes in the freezer. We are giving an example of a few various major brands and found out that all of the instructions should apply to any brand.

NOTE: Our recipes are made with the 2qt Ice Cream Bowl.

1	Always start with a clean bowl (even wash it before first use). Don't forget to wipe the freezer bowl with warm water and dish soap.
2	Freeze your bowl! We mentioned this earlier, but make sure to freeze the freezer bowl in your freezer for a minimum of 24 hours before making ice cream. Once you wash and dry your bowl but before freezing it, always wrap it in plastic wrap so it doesn't get freezer burn. Store it in the back of the freezer so it can get extra cold.
3	Combine the ingredients in the recipes in a separate container before placing them in your ice cream maker. Make sure you use a mixing container you can pour from easily.
4	With the ice cream bowl that you are using, make sure you **don't** fill the freezer bowl all the way to the top, always leave at least ½" of room. The ingredients will increase in volume so be careful not to over fill your bowl!
5	Put the freezer bowl into place on the base. Push down on the back of the bowl until the bowl pin fits snugly.
6	Pace the dasher inside the freezer bowl
7	Slide the drive assembly on the motor head until it's well connected.
8	Raise the bowl to attach the dasher to the drive assembly.
9	Turn the mixer on to Stir. The dasher will start to rotate.
10	Slowly pour your ingredients into the bowl.
11	It's ice cream making time! Allow your ice cream maker to go for 25-35 minutes depending on the recipe. Then turn off the ice cream maker and place the ice cream in another container. Put the container in the freezer for an additional 2 hours or more to set. Enjoy!

Instructions for a General Ice Cream Bucket

These basic instructions work for any electric ice cream maker bucket. For these instructions, we used a few name brands but the instructions should apply to any brand. Refer to your manual for specific instructions.

NOTE: Our recipes in this book are made to make 2qts of Ice Cream.

1	Always start with a clean ice cream maker (even wash it before your first use).
2	Combine the ingredients in the recipes in a separate container before placing them in your ice cream maker. Make sure you use a mixing container you can pour from easily.
3	The bowl is built to make no more than 4 quarts. Never fill the canister all the way to the top, fill it 2/3 full at most. The ingredients will increase the volume so be careful!
4	Pour the ingredients into the canister.
5	Secure the lid firmly onto the canister.
6	Place the canister in the middle of the bucket.
7	Assemble the motor over canister. Put the rectangle ends of the motor over the rectangular holes on the bowl's rim.
8	Always break down your ice into small pieces before using.
9	Put1 to 2 inches of ice in the bucket around the canister. Then coat with a layer of rock salt, about ½ cup. Continue alternating the ingredients until the canister has been covered.
10	Plug the machine in.
11	Make sure you stir the ice and salt about every 15 minutes while machine is churning.
12	Let the ice cream churn until the motor stops this should take about 30 minutes. Then transfer your ice cream to a different container, placing in the freezer for another 2 hours or more to set.

Delicious Ice Cream

You have to admit; ice cream will always be in style. Every flavor you can imagine you can find in this book. We even gave you just a few delicious flavors in the toppings section for you to try and experiment with. The recipes in this section will give you just a taste of what is possible. Remember to think beyond the cone!

Honey Matcha Tea Extreme Ice Cream

This macho tea extreme ice cream is definitely one you want to try. Mix it with something sweet like cookies or even honey. Yum!

Preparation Time About: 2 Hours 50 Minutes | **Servings:** 6

INGREDIENTS
2 cups heavy cream
1 cup milk
3/4 cup sugar
1 teaspoon vanilla extract
1 tablespoon Matcha
3 tablespoons organic honey

DIRECTIONS
- **NOTE: Freeze your ice cream bowl for at least 24hrs prior to starting!**
- Place the milk and cream in a bowl, and mix them together until well combined. Use a whisk to mix in the sugar. Continue to whisk for about 4 minutes until the sugar dissolves. Then mix in the vanilla extract. Finally whisk in the Matcha until well mixed.
- Pour the ingredients into your ice cream maker, and let it churn for 25 minutes.
- Put the ice cream in an airtight container and place in the freezer for around 2 hours. Allow the ice cream to thaw for 15 minutes before serving.

Tangerine Soda Ice Cream

This has all the great taste of your favorite orange soda. It's has a nice creaminess, and is oh so sweet.

Preparation Time About: 2 Hours 50 Minutes | **Servings:** 6

INGREDIENTS

2 cups heavy cream
1 cup milk
3/4 cup sugar
1 teaspoon vanilla extract
20 ounces of your favorite orange soda
orange extract (just a few drops)

DIRECTIONS

- NOTE: Freeze your ice cream bowl for at least 24hrs prior to starting!
- Place the milk and cream in a bowl, and mix them together until well combined. Use a whisk to mix in the sugar. Continue to whisk for about 4 minutes until the sugar dissolves. Then mix in the vanilla extract, orange soda and the few drops of orange extract.
- Pour the ingredients into your ice cream maker, and let it churn for 25 minutes.
- Put the ice cream in an airtight container and place in the freezer for around 2 hours. Allow the ice cream to thaw for 15 minutes before serving.

Peppermint Hibiscus Tea Ice Cream

Hibiscus tea has been known to have a lot of great benefits and peppermint is a soothing and therapeutic element. Mixed with ice cream this one should be one of your favorites!

Preparation Time About: 2 Hours 50 Minutes | **Servings:** 6

INGREDIENTS

2 cups heavy cream
1 cup milk
3/4 cup sugar
1 teaspoon vanilla extract
2 tablespoons peppermint tea
2 tablespoons hibiscus tea

DIRECTIONS

- NOTE: Freeze your ice cream bowl for at least 24hrs prior to starting!
- Put the milk in a pan and bring it to a simmer. Add in the tea, take the pot off the heat, and allow to seep for 5 minutes. Discard the tea, and allow milk to cool.
- Place the milk and cream in a bowl, and mix them together until well combined. Use a whisk to mix in the sugar. Continue to whisk for about 4 minutes until the sugar dissolves. Then mix in the vanilla extract.
- Pour the ingredients into your ice cream maker, and let it churn for 25 minutes.
- Put the ice cream in an airtight container and place in the freezer for around 2 hours. Allow the ice cream to thaw for 15 minutes before serving.

"Crispy" Caramel Graham Cracker Ice Cream

This ice cream bursting with crispy caramel loveliness thanks to the graham cracker. It gives this one just the right amount of soft crunchiness

Preparation Time About: 2 Hours 50 Minutes | **Servings:** 6

INGREDIENTS
2 cups heavy cream
1 cup milk
3/4 cup sugar
1 tablespoon vanilla extract
1 ½ cups chopped mini Kit Kats
2 oz. caramel

DIRECTIONS
- **NOTE: Freeze your ice cream bowl for at least 24hrs prior to starting!**
- Place the milk and cream in a bowl, and mix them together until well combined. Use a whisk to mix in the sugar. Continue to whisk for about 4 minutes until the sugar dissolves. Then mix in the vanilla extract.
- Warm up the caramel to add to the ice cream maker towards the end of the process.
- Pour the ingredients into your ice cream maker, and let it churn for 25 minutes. About 5 minutes before the ice cream is done churning add the graham crackers and caramel to the machine.
- Put the ice cream in an airtight container and place in the freezer for around 2 hours. Allow the ice cream to thaw for 15 minutes before serving.

"Georgia Peach" Maple Syrup Soft Serve Ice Cream

This ice cream tastes like peach Georgia peach waffles. Beautiful summer color, and is a perfect summer ice cream recipes.

Preparation Time About: 35 Minutes | **Servings:** 6

INGREDIENTS
2 cups heavy cream
1 cup milk
3/4 cup sugar
1 Tbs. vanilla extract
1 cup peaches
¼ cup maple syrup

DIRECTIONS
- **NOTE: Freeze your ice cream bowl for at least 24hrs prior to starting!**
- Puree the peaches in a food processor or blender.
- Place the milk and cream in a bowl, and mix them together until well combined. Use a whisk to mix in the sugar. Continue to whisk for about 4 minutes until the sugar dissolves. Then mix in the vanilla extract. Then mix in the blueberries, and maple syrup.
- Pour the ingredients into your ice cream maker, and let it churn for 25 minutes.
- Serve immediately.

Blueberry Mint Soft Serve Ice Cream

Here's an iced cold twist on this southern favorite. Making this dessert a minty, blueberry heavenly flavor that you will love to enjoy!

Preparation Time About: 35 Minutes | **Servings:** 6

INGREDIENTS
2 cups heavy cream
1 cup milk
3/4 cup sugar
½ cup blueberries
1 Tbs. vanilla extract
1 cup sliced peaches
1 hand full of mint leaves

DIRECTIONS
- NOTE: Freeze your ice cream bowl for at least 24hrs prior to starting!
- Puree the peaches and mint in a food processor or blender.
- Place the milk and cream in a bowl, and mix them together until well combined. Use a whisk to mix in the sugar. Continue to whisk for about 4 minutes until the sugar dissolves. Then mix in the vanilla extract, blueberries and mint.
- Pour the ingredients into your ice cream maker, and let it churn for 25 minutes.
- Serve immediately.

California Mango Lime Soft Serve Ice Cream

This recipe is a refreshing tropical mango flavor with lime on the nodes of your taste buds. It's sweet, creamy and delicious. Be sure you make enough to whip up a second batch.

Preparation Time About: 35 Minutes | **Servings:** 6

INGREDIENTS
2 cups heavy cream
1 cup milk
3/4 cup sugar
1 Tbs. vanilla extract
1 cup pureed mango (about 2.5 mangos)
Juice of 1 lime

DIRECTIONS
- NOTE: Freeze your ice cream bowl for at least 24hrs prior to starting!
- Puree the mangos with the lime juice in a food processor or blender.
- Place the milk and cream in a bowl, and mix them together until well combined. Use a whisk to mix in the sugar. Continue to whisk for about 4 minutes until the sugar dissolves. Then mix in the vanilla extract. Then mix in the mango lime puree.
- Pour the ingredients into your ice cream maker, and let it churn for 25 minutes.
- Serve immediately.

Cinnamon Blackberry Pineapple Ice Cream

Blackberry and pineapple...are you out of your mind! Twist your tongue up in this deep cinnamon richness. The concentrate is used instead of fresh grapes, all of the flavor mixed together will make you a lover of this special delight.

Preparation Time About: 2 Hours 50 Minutes | **Servings:** 6

INGREDIENTS
2 cups heavy cream
1 cup milk
3/4 cup sugar
1 teaspoon vanilla extract
½ cup pineapples
¼ cup of blackberries
1 tsp. cinnamon
juice of 1/2 lemon

DIRECTIONS
* NOTE: Freeze your ice cream bowl for at least 24hrs prior to starting!
* Place the milk and cream in a bowl, and mix them together until well combined. Use a whisk to mix in the sugar. Continue to whisk for about 4 minutes until the sugar dissolves. Then mix in the vanilla extract, pineapples, blackberries lemon juice, and cinnamon.
* Pour the ingredients into your ice cream maker, and let it churn for 25 minutes.
* Put the ice cream in an airtight container and place in the freezer for around 2 hours. Allow the ice cream to thaw for 15 minutes before serving.

Orange Almond Apricot Ice Cream

The orange flavor of this delight is as pleasing as it sounds. The almonds add a nice crunch, and a deep nutty flavor to compliment the apricots. The apricots enhance this ice cream a delicious sweet, and fresh flavor.

Preparation Time About: 2 Hours 50 Minutes | **Servings:** 6

INGREDIENTS
2 cups heavy cream
1 cup milk
3/4 cup sugar
1 teaspoon vanilla extract
1 cup sliced apricots
½ cup chopped almonds
orange extract (just a few drops will do)

DIRECTIONS
* >NOTE: Freeze your ice cream bowl for at least 24hrs prior to starting!
* Puree the apricots in a food processor or blender.
* Place the milk and cream in a bowl, and mix them together until well combined. Use a whisk to mix in the sugar. Continue to whisk for about 4 minutes until the sugar dissolves. Then mix in the vanilla extract, and apricot puree.
* Pour the ingredients into your ice cream maker, and let it churn for 25 minutes. About 5 minutes before the ice cream is finished churning, add in the almonds and orange extract.
* Put the ice cream in an airtight container and place in the freezer for around 2 hours. Allow the ice cream to thaw for 15 minutes before serving.

Kiwi Lime Strawberry Ice Cream

Did someone say tropical! Just imagine yourself out in the Caribbean but indulging this one in your very own kitchen. Perfect for summer with a twist of kiwi. Giving this ice cream a light sweet flavor that's balanced by the tanginess of the lime.

Preparation Time About: 2 Hours 50 Minutes | **Servings:** 6

INGREDIENTS

2 cups heavy cream
1 cup milk
3/4 cup sugar
1/2 teaspoon vanilla extract
½ teaspoon salt
1 kiwi, peeled
5 large strawberries chopped
Juice of one and a half limes

DIRECTIONS

- NOTE: Freeze your ice cream bowl for at least 24hrs prior to starting!
- Puree the kiwi and strawberries in a food processor or blender.
- Place the milk and cream in a bowl, and mix them together until well combined. Use a whisk to mix in the sugar and salt. Continue to whisk for about 4 minutes until the sugar and salt dissolves. Then mix in the vanilla extract, lime juice, and kiwi strawberry puree.
- Pour the ingredients into your ice cream maker, and let it churn for 25 minutes.
- Put the ice cream in an airtight container and place in the freezer for around 2 hours. Allow the ice cream to thaw for 15 minutes before serving.

Vanilla Apple Cinnamon Ice Cream

The rich flavors of this one will make you feel like you're eating apple pie. Great for fall and winter. The cinnamon heightens the flavor of the apples, and walnuts and lifts warmth from the creaminess of the ice cream.

Preparation Time About: 2 Hours 50 Minutes | **Servings:** 6

INGREDIENTS
2 cups heavy cream
1 cup milk
3/4 cup sugar
1 teaspoon vanilla extract
1 teaspoon ground cinnamon
2 large apples peeled, cored, and sliced
1/4 cup chopped walnuts

DIRECTIONS
- NOTE: Freeze your ice cream bowl for at least 24hrs prior to starting!
- Puree the apples in a food processor or blender.
- Place the milk and cream in a bowl, and mix them together until well combined. Use a whisk to mix in the sugar. Continue to whisk for about 4 minutes until the sugar dissolves. Then mix in the vanilla extract, cinnamon, and apple puree.
- Pour the ingredients into your ice cream maker, and let it churn for 25 minutes. About 5 minutes before the ice cream is finished churning, add in the walnuts and several drops of vanilla!
- Put the ice cream in an airtight container and place in the freezer for around 2 hours. Allow the ice cream to thaw for 15 minutes before serving.

Radical Rocky Road Ice Cream

This ice cream is filled with different textures thanks to the soft marshmallows, and hard nuts. The flavors combine with the chocolate to create a sweet, rich, delicious ice cream.

Preparation Time About: 2 Hours 50 Minutes | **Servings:** 6

INGREDIENTS
2 cups heavy cream
1 cup milk
3/4 cup sugar
1 Tbs. vanilla extract
½ cup unsweetened cocoa powder
½ cup chopped pecans
1 cup mini marshmallows

DIRECTIONS
- NOTE: Freeze your ice cream bowl for at least 24hrs prior to starting!
- Place the milk and cream in a bowl, and mix them together until well combined. Use a whisk to mix in the sugar. Continue to whisk for about 4 minutes until the sugar dissolves. Then whisk in cocoa powder until all lumps are gone, and well mixed. Then mix in the vanilla extract.
- Pour the ingredients into your ice cream maker, and let it churn for 25 minutes. About 5 minutes before the ice cream is finished churning, add in the pecans and marshmallows.
- Put the ice cream in an airtight container and place in the freezer for around 2 hours. Allow the ice cream to thaw for 15 minutes before serving.

All-American Double Vanilla Soft-Serve Ice Cream

Two thumbs up for this special treat! It's the classic taste you grew up with. This simple ice cream is made with only the 4 perfect ingredients, oh so delicious. Nothing says comfort like vanilla ice cream.

Preparation Time About: 35 Minutes | **Servings:** 6

INGREDIENTS

2 cups heavy cream
1 cup milk
3/4 cup sugar
2 Tbs. vanilla extract

DIRECTIONS

- NOTE: Freeze your ice cream bowl for at least 24hrs prior to starting!
- Place the milk and cream in a bowl, and mix them together until well combined. Use a whisk to mix in the sugar. Continue to whisk for about 4 minutes until the sugar dissolves. Then mix in the vanilla extract.
- Pour the ingredients into your ice cream maker, and let it churn for 25 minutes.
- Serve immediately.

Cinnamon Chocolate Chip Soft Serve Ice Cream

This Chocolate and cinnamon will have you dreaming in your sleep! Try using dark chocolate chips if you want a real contrast in flavors. The chocolate chips give a rich flavor to the delicate vanilla in the ice cream.

Preparation Time About: 35 Minutes | **Servings:** 6

INGREDIENTS

2 cups heavy cream
1 cup milk
3/4 cup sugar
1 Tbs. vanilla extract
1 cup chocolate chips of your choice
2 tsps. cinnamon

DIRECTIONS

- NOTE: Freeze your ice cream bowl for at least 24hrs prior to starting!
- Place the milk and cream in a bowl, and mix them together until well combined. Use a whisk to mix in the sugar. Continue to whisk for about 4 minutes until the sugar dissolves. Then mix in the vanilla extract.
- Pour the ingredients into your ice cream maker, and let it churn for 25 minutes. About 5 minutes before the ice cream is finished churning, add in the chocolate chips.
- Serve immediately.

Chicago Style Cookies-N-Cream Soft Serve Ice Cream

This Chicago style ice cream combines the delicious flavors of vanilla ice cream and chocolate sandwich cookies. The rich taste of the sandwich cookies is complimented by the subtle creaminess of the vanilla ice cream. This is one of my all-time classic!

Preparation Time About: 35 Minutes | **Servings:** 6

INGREDIENTS
2 cups heavy cream
1 cup milk
3/4 cup sugar
1 Tbs. vanilla extract
20 chocolate sandwich cookies
DIRECTIONS
- NOTE: Freeze your ice cream bowl for at least 24hrs prior to starting!
- Place the milk and cream in a bowl, and mix them together until well combined. Use a whisk to mix in the sugar. Continue to whisk for about 4 minutes until the sugar dissolves. Then mix in the vanilla extract.
- Place the sandwich cookies in a food processor, and process until the cookies are no bigger than chocolate chips. If you don't have a food processor place the cookies in a large resealable plastic bag, and seal it shut. Use your hands, a mallet, or a rolling pin to crush the cookies.
- Pour the ingredients into your ice cream maker, and let it churn for 25 minutes. About 5 minutes before the ice cream is finished churning, add in the chocolate sandwich cookies.
- Serve immediately.

Chocolate Chip Turmeric Peppermint Chip Ice Cream

This fresh, aromatic sweet, tasting bowl of goodness and the taste of the mint it complimented by the strong flavor of the chocolate. This classic ice cream is comfort in a bowl.

Preparation Time About: 2 Hours 50 Minutes | **Servings:** 6

INGREDIENTS
2 cups heavy cream
1 cup milk
3/4 cup sugar
1 teaspoon vanilla extract
1 teaspoon peppermint extract
1 cup semi-sweet chocolate chips
2 teaspoons turmeric
DIRECTIONS
- NOTE: Freeze your ice cream bowl for at least 24hrs prior to starting!
- Place the milk and cream in a bowl, and mix them together until well combined. Use a whisk to mix in the sugar. Continue to whisk for about 4 minutes until the sugar dissolves. Then mix in the vanilla, turmeric and peppermint extract.
- Pour the ingredients into your ice cream maker, and let it churn for 25 minutes. About 5 minutes before the ice cream is finished churning, add in the chocolate chips.
- Put the ice cream in an airtight container and place in the freezer for around 2 hours. Allow the ice cream to thaw for 15 minutes before serving.

Chocolate Pistachio Ice Cream

This flavor is one of the 3 parts of spumoni ice cream. It has a light pistachio flavor that's light, and creamy. The chocolate just kicks all of the flavor together and smacks you in the mouth with its richness!

Preparation Time About: 2 Hours 50 Minutes | **Servings:** 6

INGREDIENTS
2 cups heavy cream
1 cup milk
3/4 cup sugar
1/4 teaspoon almond extract
1/2 cup chopped pistachios
1 cup semi-sweet chocolate chips
DIRECTIONS
• NOTE: Freeze your ice cream bowl for at least 24hrs prior to starting!
• Place the milk and cream in a bowl, and mix them together until well combined. Use a whisk to mix in the sugar. Continue to whisk for about 4 minutes until the sugar dissolves. Then mix in the almond extract.
• Pour the ingredients into your ice cream maker, and let it churn for 25 minutes. About 5 minutes before the ice cream is finished churning, add in the pistachios and chocolate chips.
• Put the ice cream in an airtight container and place in the freezer for around 2 hours. Allow the ice cream to thaw for 15 minutes before serving.

Gelato

Gelato is a popular frozen dessert of Italian origin. It is generally made with a base of milk and sugar. It is generally lower in fat than other styles of frozen desserts.

This section if filled with the succulent sweet flavors of the most delicious flavors you can handle. Sit back and enjoy, the best is yet to come!

Cherry Chocolate Pretzel Gelato

Did someone say Cherry Chocolate? The pretzels give the gelato a lovely, crunchy saltiness that enhance and balance the chocolate. This favorite of ours has the chocolaty deeply richness as a base for the gelato.

Preparation Time About: 2 Hours 35 Minutes | **Servings:** 4-6

INGREDIENTS
1/2 cup heavy cream
2 cups milk
3/4 cup sugar
1 teaspoon vanilla extract
2 ounces pitted cherries
3 ounces semi-sweet chocolate
4 ounce pretzels

DIRECTIONS
- NOTE: Freeze your ice cream bowl for at least 24hrs prior to starting!
- Melt the chocolate, and allow it to cool a little bit.
- Place the milk and cream in a bowl, and mix them together until well combined. Use a whisk to mix in the sugar. Continue to whisk for about 4 minutes until the sugar dissolves. Then mix in the vanilla extract. Finally mix in the chocolate and cherries.
- Place the pretzels in a food processor, and process until the cookies are no bigger than chocolate chips. If you don't have a food processor place the pretzels in a large resealable plastic bag, and seal it shut. Use your hands, a mallet, or a rolling pin to crush the pretzels.
- Pour the ingredients into your ice cream maker, and let it churn for 25 minutes. About 5 minutes before the ice cream is done churning add the pretzels to your ice cream maker.

Put the gelato in an airtight container and place in the freezer for up to 2 hours, until desired consistency is reached.

Chocolate Matcha Gelato

The chocolate in this one helps to cut through the flavor of the Matcha, and adds a deep flavor with the chocolate. The Matcha has an intense green tea flavor. It's a flavor to indulge every time.

Preparation Time About: 2 Hours 35 Minutes | **Servings:** 4-6

INGREDIENTS
1/2 cup heavy cream
2 cups milk
3/4 cup sugar
1 teaspoon vanilla extract
1 tablespoon Matcha
2 ounces chopped dark chocolate

DIRECTIONS
- 〉NOTE: Freeze your ice cream bowl for at least 24hrs prior to starting!
- Place the milk and cream in a bowl, and mix them together until well combined. Use a whisk to mix in the sugar. Continue to whisk for about 4 minutes until the sugar dissolves. Then mix in the vanilla extract. Finally whisk in the Matcha until well mixed.
- Pour the ingredients into your ice cream maker, and let it churn for 25 minutes. About 5 minutes before the ice cream is done churning add the chocolate to your ice cream maker.
- Put the gelato in an airtight container and place in the freezer for up to 2 hours, until desired consistency is reached.

Kiwi Strawberry Gelato

This ice cream treat goes really well with a nice piece of chocolate cake. This gelato has an intense strawberry flavor. Something you want to share with that special someone.

Preparation Time About: 2 Hours 35 Minutes | **Servings:** 4-6

INGREDIENTS
1/2 cup heavy cream
2 cups milk
3/4 cup sugar
1/2 cup sliced strawberries
1/2 cup finely chopped kiwi
1 tablespoon vanilla extract

DIRECTIONS
- **NOTE: Freeze your ice cream bowl for at least 24hrs prior to starting!**
- Puree the strawberries in a food processor or blender.
- Place the milk and cream in a bowl, and mix them together until well combined. Use a whisk to mix in the sugar. Continue to whisk for about 4 minutes until the sugar dissolves. Then mix in the vanilla extract and strawberry puree along with the finely chopped kiwi.
- Pour the ingredients into your ice cream maker, and let it churn for 25 minutes.
- Put the gelato in an airtight container and place in the freezer for up to 2 hours, until desired consistency is reached.

Double Fudge Chocolate Gelato

This sinfully chocolaty flavor, I hope you can handle. It has a richness and dense chocolate flavor that chocoholics will crave! And when you say double fudge, everyone will come running.

Preparation Time About: 2 Hours 35 Minutes | **Servings:** 4-6

INGREDIENTS
1/2 cup heavy cream
2 cups milk
3/4 cup sugar
1/4 teaspoon salt
7 ounces high quality dark chocolate fudge
1 teaspoon vanilla extract

DIRECTIONS
- NOTE: Freeze your ice cream bowl for at least 24hrs prior to starting!
- Melt the chocolate, and allow it to cool a little bit.
- Place the milk and cream in a bowl, and mix them together until well combined. Use a whisk to mix in the sugar and salt. Continue to whisk for about 4 minutes until the sugar and salt dissolve. Then mix in the vanilla extract. Finally mix in the fudge until well combined.
- Pour the ingredients into your ice cream maker, and let it churn for 25 minutes.
- Put the gelato in an airtight container and place in the freezer for up to 2 hours, until desired consistency is reached.

Lemon Scented Rose Gelato

The rose pairs well with the milk and cream, and creates a delicious gelato that gives off the most delicious scent. This gelato has a romantic floral flavor.

Preparation Time About: 2 Hours 35 Minutes | **Servings:** 4-6

INGREDIENTS
1/2 cup heavy cream
2 cups milk
3/4 cup sugar
1 teaspoon rose extract
juice of ½ lemon

DIRECTIONS
- NOTE: Freeze your ice cream bowl for at least 24hrs prior to starting!
- Place the milk and cream in a bowl, and mix them together until well combined. Use a whisk to mix in the sugar. Continue to whisk for about 4 minutes until the sugar dissolves. Then mix in the rose extract.
- Pour the ingredients into your ice cream maker, and let it churn for 25 minutes.
- Put the gelato in an airtight container and place in the freezer for up to 2 hours, until desired consistency is reached.

Banana Pineapple Coconut Gelato

This is another tropical delight indeed! The walnuts give the gelato crunchiness, and give it a nice richness and the gelato has a full banana flavor that's not too sweet.

Preparation Time About: 2 Hours 35 Minutes | **Servings:** 4-6

INGREDIENTS
1/2 cup heavy cream
2 cups milk
3/4 cup sugar
1 tablespoon vanilla extract
½ cup sliced banana
½ cup chopped pineapple
½ cup chopped coconut
DIRECTIONS
* NOTE: Freeze your ice cream bowl for at least 24hrs prior to starting!
* Puree the bananas in a food processor or blender.
* Place the milk and cream in a bowl, and mix them together until well combined. Use a whisk to mix in the sugar. Continue to whisk for about 4 minutes until the sugar dissolves. Then mix in the vanilla extract and banana puree.
* Pour the ingredients into your ice cream maker, and let it churn for 25 minutes. About 5 minutes before the ice cream is done churning add the walnuts to your ice cream maker.
* Put the gelato in an airtight container and place in the freezer for up to 2 hours, until desired consistency is reached.

Honey Peach Gelato

Hope you have a sweet tooth, this one is peachy sweet! The apricot gives this gelato a sweet and tart flavor. The honey gives a light flavor that helps cut through the tartness of the apricot. Heavenly bliss and two thumbs up!

Preparation Time About: 2 Hours 35 Minutes | **Servings:** 4-6

INGREDIENTS
1/2 cup heavy cream
2 cups milk
3/4 cup sugar
1 cup sliced peaches
1 tablespoon vanilla extract
1/4 cup honey
DIRECTIONS
* NOTE: Freeze your ice cream bowl for at least 24hrs prior to starting!
* Puree the peaches in a food processor or blender.
* Place the milk and cream in a bowl, and mix them together until well combined. Use a whisk to mix in the sugar. Continue to whisk for about 4 minutes until the sugar dissolves. Then mix in the vanilla extract honey and peach puree.
* Pour the ingredients into your ice cream maker, and let it churn for 25 minutes.
* Put the gelato in an airtight container and place in the freezer for up to 2 hours, until desired consistency is reached.

Black Cherry Kiwi Cotton Candy Gelato

Better call the kids for this one! This chocolaty rich, complex flavor that's balanced by the sweetness of the blueberries. The gelato texture has a great balance of rich and sweet flavors.

Preparation Time About: 2 Hours 35 Minutes | **Servings:** 4-6

INGREDIENTS
1/2 cup heavy cream
2 cups milk
3/4 cup sugar
1 teaspoon vanilla extract
1 teaspoon cotton candy extract
1 cup black cherries
½ cup finely chopped kiwi
DIRECTIONS
- NOTE: Freeze your ice cream bowl for at least 24hrs prior to starting!
- Puree the apples in a food processor or blender.
- Place the milk and cream in a bowl, and mix them together until well combined. Use a whisk to mix in the sugar. Continue to whisk for about 4 minutes until the sugar dissolves. Then mix in the vanilla extract and black cherry puree.
- Pour the ingredients into your ice cream maker, and let it churn for 25 minutes. About 5 minutes before the ice cream is done churning add the kiwi to your ice cream maker.
- Put the gelato in an airtight container and place in the freezer for up to 2 hours, until desired consistency is reached.

Apple Chocolate Gelato

This gelato and apple flavor has a great balance of rich and sweet flavors. The chocolate has a rich, complex flavor that's balanced by the sweetness of the apples, and carries on throughout each spoonful of the bowl.

Preparation Time About: 2 Hours 35 Minutes | **Servings:** 4-6

INGREDIENTS
1/2 cup heavy cream
2 cups milk
3/4 cup sugar
1 teaspoon vanilla extract
1 cup apples
½ cup finely chopped semi-sweet chocolate
DIRECTIONS
- NOTE: Freeze your ice cream bowl for at least 24hrs prior to starting!
- Puree the apples in a food processor or blender.
- Place the milk and cream in a bowl, and mix them together until well combined. Use a whisk to mix in the sugar. Continue to whisk for about 4 minutes until the sugar dissolves. Then mix in the vanilla extract and apple puree.
- Pour the ingredients into your ice cream maker, and let it churn for 25 minutes. About 5 minutes before the ice cream is done churning add the chocolate to your ice cream maker.
- Put the gelato in an airtight container and place in the freezer for up to 2 hours, until desired consistency is reached.

Cinnamon Coconut Lemon Blackberry Gelato

Tropical coconut and cinnamon is the way to go. This gelato has an intense strawberry flavor. It goes really well with a nice piece of chocolate cake. Great for anytime of the year and popular to share with anyone!

Preparation Time About: 2 Hours 35 Minutes | **Servings:** 4-6

INGREDIENTS
1/2 cup heavy cream
2 cups milk
3/4 cup sugar
1/2 cup sliced Coconut
1/2 cup finely chopped Blackberries
1 tablespoon vanilla extract
1 teaspoon lemon
1 teaspoon cinnamon

DIRECTIONS
- NOTE: Freeze your ice cream bowl for at least 24hrs prior to starting!
- Puree the strawberries in a food processor or blender.
- Place the milk and cream in a bowl, and mix them together until well combined. Use a whisk to mix in the sugar. Continue to whisk for about 4 minutes until the sugar dissolves. Then mix in the vanilla extract, cinnamon, lemon, blackberry puree along with the finely chopped coconut.
- Pour the ingredients into your ice cream maker, and let it churn for 25 minutes.
- Put the gelato in an airtight container and place in the freezer for up to 2 hours, until desired consistency is reached.

Delicious Fro Yo!

Delicious Fro Yo is some of the best tasting dessert on the market. You can possibly combine any flavor you like into this amazingly delicious frozen treat. In this section, you will be creating some heavenly deliciousness for your friends and family to enjoy.

White Chocolate Chip Cookie Dough Frozen Yogurt

If you're not a white chocolate chip lover, then you will be after this! The sweet flavors of cookie dough and chocolate take center stage in this classic. The yogurt has a creamy richness to the vanilla base that lets the cookie dough to shine with every mouthful.

Preparation Time About: 2 Hours 35 Minutes | **Servings:** 1 Quart

INGREDIENTS

1 quart container full-fat plain yogurt
¼ teaspoon salt
1 cup sugar
1 tablespoon vanilla extract
½ cup prepackaged cookie dough cut into small chunks
½ cup finely chopped white chocolate chips

DIRECTIONS

- **NOTE: Freeze your ice cream bowl for at least 24hrs prior to starting!**
- Place the yogurt in a bowl. Use a whisk to mix in the sugar and salt. Continue to whisk for about 4 minutes until the sugar dissolves. Then mix in the vanilla extract.
- Pour the ingredients into your ice cream maker, and let it churn for 25 minutes. About 5 minutes before the ice cream is done churning add the cookie dough and white chocolate to your ice cream maker.
- Put the frozen yogurt in an airtight container and place in the freezer for at least 2 hours, until desired consistency is reached.

Cinnamon Clove Coffee Frozen Yogurt

You never thought you would mix cloves in with ice cream, did you. Well... you'd better use decaf coffee if you don't want a coffee buzz! This one makes a great pick me up on a hot summer day instead of regular coffee.

Preparation Time About: 2 Hours 35 Minutes | **Servings:** 1.5 Quarts

INGREDIENTS
1 quart container full-fat plain yogurt
¼ teaspoon salt
1 cup sugar
2 teaspoons cinnamon
1 tablespoon cloves pulverized
1 teaspoon vanilla extract
1 cup strong brewed coffee or espresso
1 tablespoon coffee grounds
DIRECTIONS
* NOTE: Freeze your ice cream bowl for at least 24hrs prior to starting!
* Place the yogurt in a bowl. Use a whisk to mix in the sugar and salt. Continue to whisk for about 4 minutes until the sugar dissolves. Then mix in the vanilla extract, coffee, and coffee grounds, cloves and cinnamon.
* Pour the ingredients into your ice cream maker, and let it churn for 25 minutes.
* Put the frozen yogurt in an airtight container and place in the freezer for at least 2 hours, until desired consistency is reached.

Berry Pumpkin Spice Frozen Yogurt

I love pumpkin spice, but mixing berry flavor with it? This makes for a very flavorful bowl of absolute deliciousness. This one is what we call the tongue twister of flavor in every scoop.

Preparation Time About: 2 Hours 35 Minutes | **Servings:** 1.5 Quarts

INGREDIENTS
1 quart container full-fat plain yogurt
¼ teaspoon salt
1 cup sugar
1 tablespoon vanilla extract
1 cup raspberries
1 cup blueberries
2 tablespoons pumpkin spice
DIRECTIONS
* NOTE: Freeze your ice cream bowl for at least 24hrs prior to starting!
* Puree the raspberries, blueberries and pumpkin spice in a food processor or blender
* Place the yogurt in a bowl. Use a whisk to mix in the sugar and salt. Continue to whisk for about 4 minutes until the sugar dissolves. Then mix in the vanilla extract, berry and pumpkin spice puree.
* Pour the ingredients into your ice cream maker, and let it churn for 25 minutes.
* Put the frozen yogurt in an airtight container and place in the freezer for at least 2 hours, until desired consistency is reached.

White Chocolate Citrus Rose Frozen Yogurt

The rose water lightly enhances the frozen yogurt with a touch of floral flavor, along with. This frozen yogurt as a light sweet flavor thanks to the white chocolate.

Preparation Time About: 2 Hours 35 Minutes | **Servings:** 1 Quart

INGREDIENTS
1 quart container full-fat plain yogurt
¼ teaspoon salt
1 cup sugar
1 teaspoon vanilla extract
6 ounces chopped white chocolate
½ teaspoon citrus extract
½ teaspoon rose water

DIRECTIONS
- NOTE: Freeze your ice cream bowl for at least 24hrs prior to starting!
- Melt the white chocolate and let it cool a bit
- Place the yogurt in a bowl. Use a whisk to mix in the sugar and salt. Continue to whisk for about 4 minutes until the sugar dissolves. Then mix in the vanilla extract, rose water, citrus extract and white chocolate.
- Pour the ingredients into your ice cream maker, and let it churn for 25 minutes.
- Put the frozen yogurt in an airtight container and place in the freezer for at least 2 hours, until desired consistency is reached.

Chocolate Bacon Frozen Yogurt

You may not think of bacon as something that goes in dessert, but it adds a nice salty bacon flavor, to this creamy chocolate texture. Make sure to make enough for seconds for everyone.

Preparation Time About: 2 Hours 35 Minutes | **Servings:** 1 Quart

INGREDIENTS
1 quart container full-fat plain yogurt
¼ teaspoon salt
1 cup sugar
1 teaspoon vanilla extract
4 ounces chopped dark chocolate
½ cup olive oil
½ cup crispy bacon

DIRECTIONS
- NOTE: Freeze your ice cream bowl for at least 24hrs prior to starting!
- Place the yogurt in a bowl. Use a whisk to mix in the sugar and salt. Continue to whisk for about 4 minutes until the sugar dissolves. Then mix in the vanilla extract, olive oil and bacon.
- Pour the ingredients into your ice cream maker, and let it churn for 25 minutes. About 5 minutes before the ice cream is done churning add the chocolate to your ice cream maker.
- Put the frozen yogurt in an airtight container and place in the freezer for at least 2 hours, until desired consistency is reached.

Pumpkin Cinnamon Raisin Gingerbread Frozen Yogurt

This has all the flavor of wintertime. The ginger and cinnamon give this frozen yogurt a lovely warm flavor, along with the pumpkin and molasses extracting out of the gingerbread.

Preparation Time About: 2 Hours 35 Minutes | **Servings:** 1 Quart

INGREDIENTS
1 quart container full-fat plain yogurt
¼ teaspoon salt
1 cup sugar
1 teaspoon vanilla extract
1/2 cup pumpkin
¼ cup raisins
2 tablespoons molasses
1 teaspoon cinnamon
¼ teaspoon ginger
DIRECTIONS
- NOTE: Freeze your ice cream bowl for at least 24hrs prior to starting!
- Place all the ingredients in a blender and blend on high until pureed and sugar dissolves.
- Pour the ingredients into your ice cream maker, and let it churn for 25 minutes. About 5 minutes before the ice cream is done churning add the raisins to your ice cream maker.
- Put the frozen yogurt in an airtight container and place in the freezer for at least 2 hours, until desired consistency is reached.

Walnut Mint Pomegranate Frozen Yogurt

This yogurt has a rich full flavor thanks to the nuttiness of the walnuts, the sweetness of the pomegranate, and freshness of the mint. Use less mint extract if you want a more robust pomegranate flavor.

Preparation Time About: 2 Hours 35 Minutes | **Servings:** 1 Quart

INGREDIENTS
1 quart container full-fat plain yogurt
¼ teaspoon salt
1 cup sugar
1 tablespoon mint extract
1 cup 100% pomegranate juice
1/2 cup walnuts
DIRECTIONS
- NOTE: Freeze your ice cream bowl for at least 24hrs prior to starting!
- Place the yogurt in a bowl. Use a whisk to mix in the sugar and salt. Continue to whisk for about 4 minutes until the sugar dissolves. Then mix in the mint extract, and pomegranate juice.
- Pour the ingredients into your ice cream maker, and let it churn for 25 minutes. About 5 minutes before the ice cream is done churning add the chocolate chips to your ice cream maker.
- Put the frozen yogurt in an airtight container and place in the freezer for at least 2 hours, until desired consistency is reached.

Brown Sugar Honey Mango Frozen Yogurt

Mango just screams summertime, and childhood for a most of you out there. The brown sugar and honey flavor is enhanced by the sweetness, to the rich creamy taste or the yogurt.

Preparation Time About: 2 Hours 35 Minutes | **Servings:** 1 Quart

INGREDIENTS
1 quart container full-fat plain yogurt
¼ teaspoon salt
1 cup sugar
1 teaspoon vanilla extract
8 ounces mango
1/4 cup honey
2 tablespoons brown sugar

DIRECTIONS
- **NOTE: Freeze your ice cream bowl for at least 24hrs prior to starting!**
- Puree the strawberries in a food processor or blender.
- Place the yogurt in a bowl. Use a whisk to mix in the sugar and salt. Continue to whisk for about 4 minutes until the sugar dissolves. Then mix in the vanilla extract, honey, brown sugar and mango puree.
- Pour the ingredients into your ice cream maker, and let it churn for 25 minutes.
- Put the frozen yogurt in an airtight container and place in the freezer for at least 2 hours, until desired consistency is reached.

Silk Shakes

Milkshake madness is on the menu. We give you a nice variety of flavors to have as an after-dinner delight. Cancel going to the movies and turn on the television and snuggle up to a little something like a succulent "Silkshake!" Get creative and show off that imagination, and enjoy!

Lemon Lime Soda Milkshake

This is a great lemon-lime flavor that is a little tangy and refreshing. The natural version of sprite in milkshake form make this one loved by anyone who gets a whiff of this delicious dessert and indulges.

Preparation Time About: 25 Minutes | **Servings:** 6

INGREDIENTS
2 cups heavy cream
1 cup milk
3/4 cup sugar
1 teaspoon vanilla extract
¼ cup lime juice
¼ cup lemon juice
¼ cup 7up or Sprite
Zest of one lemon
Zest of one lime

DIRECTIONS
- NOTE: Freeze your ice cream bowl for at least 24hrs prior to starting!
- Place the milk and cream in a bowl, and mix them together until well combined. Use a whisk to mix in the sugar. Continue to whisk for about 4 minutes until the sugar dissolves. Then mix in the vanilla extract, juice, Sprite/7-Up and zest.
- Pour the ingredients into your ice cream maker, and let it churn for 10-15 minutes, until desired consistency is reached.
- Serve immediately.

Caramel & Pistachio Milkshake

When making this one, make sure you chop your pistachios small enough to fit through a straw. A blender works well in doing this. This classic milkshake combines creamy ice cream with rich caramel sweet flavor and the over tones of pistachios.

Preparation Time About: 25 Minutes | **Servings:** 6

INGREDIENTS
2 cups heavy cream
1 cup milk
1 cup brown sugar
1 teaspoon vanilla extract
2 ounces caramel
1/3 cup finely chopped pistachios
1 tablespoon butter

DIRECTIONS
- **NOTE: Freeze your ice cream bowl for at least 24hrs prior to starting!**
- Melt the butter in a small skillet on medium heat. Add the Pistachios, and cook for about 5 minutes, until they become lightly browned.
- Place the milk and cream in a bowl, and mix them together until well combined. Use a whisk to mix in the sugar. Continue to whisk for about 4 minutes until the sugar dissolves. Then mix in the vanilla extract.
- Pour the ingredients into your ice cream maker, and let it churn for 10-15 minutes, until desired consistency is reached. About 5 minutes before the ice cream is done churning add the caramel to your ice cream maker.

Mint Cookies 'N Sea Salt "Silkshake"

Creamy and minty! This a twist of two classic ice cream flavors. You get the flavor of mint with the cookie texture of cookies 'n cream. This one will make a great ice cream sandwich indeed!

Preparation Time About: 25 Minutes | **Servings:** 6

INGREDIENTS
2 cups heavy cream
1 cup milk
3/4 cup sugar
1 teaspoon sea salt
1 teaspoon vanilla extract
1 ½ teaspoons mint extract
10 chocolate sandwich cookies

DIRECTIONS
- **Freeze bowl (Refer to note on page XX about freezing bowl)**
- Place the milk and cream in a bowl, and mix them together until well combined. Use a whisk to mix in the sugar. Continue to whisk for about 4 minutes until the sugar dissolves. Then mix in the vanilla, sea salt and mint extract.
- Place the sandwich cookies in a food processor, and process until the cookies are finely processed. If you don't have a food processor place the cookies in a large resealable plastic bag, and seal it shut. Use your hands, a mallet, or a rolling pin to crush the cookies.
- Pour the ingredients into your ice cream maker, and let it churn for 10-15 minutes, until desired consistency is reached. About 5 minutes before the ice cream is done churning add the cookies to your ice cream maker.

Cherry Pineapple Chocolate Milkshake

This is a natural version of sprite in milkshake form. The lemon and lime flavors are tangy and refreshing.

Preparation Time About: 25 Minutes | **Servings:** 6

INGREDIENTS
2 cups heavy cream
1 cup milk
3/4 cup sugar
1 teaspoon vanilla extract
¼ cup pineapples
1 cup cherry juice
¼ cup semi-sweet chocolate chips

DIRECTIONS
- NOTE: Freeze your ice cream bowl for at least 24hrs prior to starting!
- Place the milk and cream in a bowl, and mix them together until well combined. Use a whisk to mix in the sugar. Continue to whisk for about 4 minutes until the sugar dissolves. Then mix in the vanilla extract, and cherry juice.
- Pour the ingredients into your ice cream maker, and let it churn for 10-15 minutes, until desired consistency is reached. About 5 minutes before the ice cream is finished churning, add in the pineapples and chocolate chips.

Mint Guava Milkshake

This is a natural version of sprite in milkshake form. The lemon and lime flavors are tangy and refreshing.

Preparation Time About: 25 Minutes | **Servings:** 6

INGREDIENTS
2 cups heavy cream
1 cup milk
3/4 cup sugar
1 teaspoon vanilla extract
½ cup mint (pulverized)
1/2 cups guava juice

DIRECTIONS
- NOTE: Freeze your ice cream bowl for at least 24hrs prior to starting!
- Place the milk and cream in a bowl, and mix them together until well combined. Use a whisk to mix in the sugar. Continue to whisk for about 4 minutes until the sugar dissolves. Then mix in the vanilla extract, and juice.
- Pour the ingredients into your ice cream maker, and let it churn for 10-15 minutes, until desired consistency is reached.
- Serve immediately.

Honey Mint Heaven Milkshake

This milkshake has a delicate flavor that lets the honey take center stage. The lavender gives a subtle floral flower.

Preparation Time About: 25 Minutes | **Servings:** 6

INGREDIENTS

2 cups heavy cream
1 cup milk
3/4 cup sugar
1½ teaspoon mint extract
1/3 cup honey

DIRECTIONS

- NOTE: Freeze your ice cream bowl for at least 24hrs prior to starting!
- Place the milk and cream in a bowl, and mix them together until well combined. Use a whisk to mix in the sugar. Continue to whisk for about 4 minutes until the sugar dissolves. Then mix in the mint extract, and honey.
- Pour the ingredients into your ice cream maker, and let it churn for 10-15 minutes, until desired consistency is reached.
- Serve immediately.

Cherry Fig Mint Milkshake

This is a great way to use figs when they're in season. The sweet flavor of the figs is enhanced by the fresh flavor of the mint.

Preparation Time About: 25 Minutes | **Servings:** 6

INGREDIENTS

2 cups heavy cream
1 cup milk
3/4 cup sugar
2 teaspoons vanilla extract
¼ cup lemon juice
¼ cup cherries
2 cups peeled, diced figs
2 teaspoons chopped fresh mint

DIRECTIONS

- NOTE: Freeze your ice cream bowl for at least 24hrs prior to starting!
- Place the milk and cream in a bowl, and mix them together until well combined. Use a whisk to mix in the sugar. Continue to whisk for about 4 minutes until the sugar dissolves. Then mix in the vanilla extract, lemon juice, cherries and mint.
- Pour the ingredients into your ice cream maker, and let it churn for 10-15 minutes, until desired consistency is reached. About 5 minutes before the ice cream is done churning add the figs to your ice cream maker.
- Serve immediately.

Cinnamon Maple Bacon Milkshake

Does bacon go great with ice cream? Yes, it does!! The ice cream itself has a lovely maple syrup flavor the goes well with the chunks of bacon. Bacon lovers will go crazy for this shake, especially with the cinnamon to twist the flavor.

Preparation Time About: 25 Minutes | **Servings:** 6

INGREDIENTS
2 cups heavy cream
1 cup milk
3/4 cup sugar
1 teaspoon cinnamon
1 teaspoons vanilla extract
6 slices finely chopped cooked thick cut bacon
½ cup maple syrup

DIRECTIONS
- **NOTE: Freeze your ice cream bowl for at least 24hrs prior to starting!**
- Place the milk and cream in a bowl, and mix them together until well combined. Use a whisk to mix in the sugar. Continue to whisk for about 4 minutes until the sugar dissolves. Then mix in the vanilla extract, cinnamon and maple syrup.
- Pour the ingredients into your ice cream maker, and let it churn for 10-15 minutes, until desired consistency is reached. About 5 minutes before the ice cream is done churning add the bacon to your ice cream maker.
- Serve immediately.

Succulent Sorbets

Sorbet has to be most delightful desserts and very famous with most high-end restaurants around the world. Savor the flavor of some of these elegant and delightful treats. Invite your friends and family over and enjoy the day that you opened this book and found this section for you to enjoy!

Caribbean Pineapple Mint Sorbet

Try serving it for dessert after a fish dinner or teriyaki or sweet-n-sour chicken. This sorbet is perfect when you want to cool down on a hot day, the pineapple is incredibly refreshing.

Preparation Time About: 2 hours 40 Minutes | **Servings:** 9

INGREDIENTS

1 diced, peeled, and cored small pineapple
2 tablespoons lemon juice
½ cup mint
1 cup plus 2 tablespoons sugar

DIRECTIONS

- NOTE: Freeze your ice cream bowl for at least 24hrs prior to starting!
- Puree the pineapple, mint and lemon juice in a food processor or blender. Then add in the sugar and puree until the sugar dissolves.
- Pour the ingredients into your ice cream maker, and let it churn for 25-30 minutes.
- Place in an airtight container for up to 2 hours, until desired consistency is reached.

Peanut Butter Plum Sorbet

Try combining different types of plums to make a more complex flavor to go with the peanut butter. The plums give this sorbet an interesting sweet yet tart flavor. 5 ingredients, and yummy!

Preparation Time About: 4 hours 35 Minutes | **Servings:** Makes 1 Quart

INGREDIENTS

2 pounds pitted, quartered plums
1 tablespoon light corn syrup
3 tablespoons peanut butter
1 cup sugar
¼ teaspoon salt

DIRECTIONS

- **NOTE: Freeze your ice cream bowl for at least 24hrs prior to starting!**
- Use a food processor or blender to puree the plums. Put in the sugar and corn syrup, and process for about another 30 seconds. Then blend in the salt and peanut butter. Strain the mixture into a bowl, and refrigerate covered for 2-3 hours.
- Pour the ingredients into your ice cream maker, and let it churn for 25-30 minutes.
- Place in an airtight container for up to 2 hours, until desired consistency is reached.

Black Raspberry Clementine Sorbet

This sorbet has a beautiful orange color. The sweet taste of the clementine sorbet taste best the day it's made. The flavors are married together twisting your tongue with a bliss of happiness

Preparation Time About: 4 hours 35 Minutes | **Servings:** Makes 1 Quart

INGREDIENTS

20 chilled, peeled, and segmented clementine's
½ cup Black Raspberries
1 cup sugar
¼ teaspoon salt

DIRECTIONS

- **NOTE: Freeze your ice cream bowl for at least 24hrs prior to starting!**
- Use a food processor or blender to puree the Clementine's and black raspberries. Strain the puree until you have 4 ½ cups of juice. Place the juice and sugar back in the blender or food processor. Process until sugar dissolves. Then pulse in the salt until combined.
- Pour the ingredients into your ice cream maker, and let it churn for 25-30 minutes.
- Place in an airtight container for up to 2 hours, until desired consistency is reached.

Raspberry Lavender Sorbet

This sorbet has a hint of floral flavor from the lavender and a lovely tart flavor. If the base seems a little too sour know that it will mellow or be made more, subtle a bit when it's frozen and marinades in its flavors.

Preparation Time About: 5 hours 35 Minutes | **Servings:** 6

INGREDIENTS

3 cups, mashed raspberries
½ teaspoon lavender
3/4 cup sugar
1/2 teaspoon salt
2 tablespoons vanilla extract
2 ½ teaspoons lime juice

DIRECTIONS

- NOTE: Freeze your ice cream bowl for at least 24hrs prior to starting!
- Use a food processor or blender to puree the lavender, sugar, raspberries, and vanilla extract. Then blend in the salt and lime juice. Strain the mixture into a bowl, and refrigerate covered for 2-3 hours.
- Pour the ingredients into your ice cream maker, and let it churn for 25-30 minutes. Place in an airtight container for up to 2 hours, until desired consistency is reached.

Chili Lime Mango Sorbet

This sorbet combines the mango and gives it a sweet creamy flavor. The three different flavors that go so well together with the lime adds some tartness, and the chili powder adds just a little heat.

Preparation Time About: 2 hours 40 Minutes | **Servings:** 6-8

INGREDIENTS

3 peeled, pitted, and diced large mangos
2 cups simple syrup
1/4 cup fresh lime juice
1 tablespoon chili powder
Pinch of salt

DIRECTIONS

- NOTE: Freeze your ice cream bowl for at least 24hrs prior to starting!
- Puree the mangos in a food processor or blender. Then add in the remaining ingredients and blend on low until combined.
- Pour the ingredients into your ice cream maker, and let it churn for 25-30 minutes. Place in an airtight container for up to 2 hours, until desired consistency is reached.

Lemon Mint Melon Sorbet

This sorbet is a combination of a minty, tangy sweetness that give this one a flavor you will remember for a lifetime!

Preparation Time About: 3 hours 10 Minutes | **Servings:** 4

INGREDIENTS
½ cup lemon juice
1 cup boiling water
1 cup chopped mint
½ cup melon
Zest of 1 lemon
1 cup sugar

DIRECTIONS
- **NOTE: Freeze your ice cream bowl for at least 24hrs prior to starting!**
- Mix together the sugar, lemon zest, mint and melon in a heat safe bowl. Then pour in the water, and stir frequently until sugar dissolves. Let the mixture sit for 20 minutes. Then strain it into another bowl. Mix in the lemon juice and let the mixture cool totally.
- Pour the ingredients into your ice cream maker, and let it churn for 25-30 minutes.
- Place in an airtight container for up to 2 hours, until desired consistency is reached.

Coconut Guava Raspberry Sorbet

The guava and coconut give this sorbet a lovely creaminess. The raspberries give this tropical sorbet a nice tartness. An elegant style of tropical goodness to enjoy.

Preparation Time About: 5 hours 35 Minutes | **Servings:** 6

INGREDIENTS
3 cups packed, cubed guava
1 cup fresh raspberries
1 cup full-fat coconut milk
1 cup sugar
Pinch of salt
1 teaspoon lime juice
DIRECTIONS
- NOTE: Freeze your ice cream bowl for at least 24hrs prior to starting!
- Puree all the ingredients in a food processor or blender. Then transfer the mixture to a bowl, and refrigerate covered for 3-4 hours.
- Pour the ingredients into your ice cream maker, and let it churn for 25-30 minutes.
- Place in an airtight container for up to 2 hours, until desired consistency is reached.

Amazing Key Lime Sorbet

You can't go wrong with key lime dessert. This has all the great flavor of key lime pie. This sorbet has a nice mix of sweet and tart. We say, a little key lime goodness.

Preparation Time About: 3 hours | **Servings:** 4

INGREDIENTS
3 cups cold water
2 ¼ cup fresh key lime juice
2 3/4 cup sugar
1 tablespoon lime zest
DIRECTIONS
- NOTE: Freeze your ice cream bowl for at least 24hrs prior to starting!
- Mix together the water and sugar in a large sauce pan on medium heat. Allow the mixture to come to a boil. Then lower to low heat, and let the mixture simmer until the sugar dissolve. Allow the mixture to cool completely.
- Mix the lime juice and zest with the cooled mixture.
- Pour the ingredients into your ice cream maker, and let it churn for 25-30 minutes.
- Place in an airtight container for up to 2 hours, until desired consistency is reached.

Chunky Cherry Apple Sorbet

This delightful dessert gives the taste of down home country goodness! This sorbet lets the tart sweetness of the cherries shine along with the sweet apple to complement its taste. It goes great with angel food or pound cake.

Preparation Time About: 2 hours 40 Minutes | **Servings:** 6

INGREDIENTS

6 cups frozen pitted cherries
1 apple
1/4 cup sugar
Juice of one lemon

DIRECTIONS

- NOTE: Freeze your ice cream bowl for at least 24hrs prior to starting!
- Puree the sugar, cherries and apple in a food processor or blender until smooth. Put in the lemon juice and pulse a few times to mix the ingredients.
- Pour the ingredients into your ice cream maker, and let it churn for 25-30 minutes.
- Place in an airtight container for up to 2 hours, until desired consistency is reached.

Strawberry Lime Sorbet

This sorbet has the sweetness of the strawberries and is tamed by the citrus flavor of the lime. This is a lovely velvety texture and a great dessert for you to enjoy.

Preparation Time About: 3 hours | **Servings:** 4

INGREDIENTS

2 cups water
3 pounds chilled strawberries
2 ½ cup sugar
5 chilled limes

DIRECTIONS

- NOTE: Freeze your ice cream bowl for at least 24hrs prior to starting!
- Mix together the water and sugar in a large sauce pan on medium heat. Allow the mixture to come to a boil. Then lower to low heat, and let the mixture simmer until the sugar dissolve. Allow the mixture to cool completely.
- Puree the strawberries in a food processor or blender until smooth. Then add the zest of 3 limes, juice of 5 limes, and the cooled syrup. Blend until all ingredients are mixed.
- Mix the lime juice and zest with the cooled mixture.
- Pour the ingredients into your ice cream maker, and let it churn for 25-30 minutes.
- Place in an airtight container for up to 2 hours, until desired consistency is reached.

Agave Lemon Chocolate Sorbet

If you've never tasted agave, then this one is for you! Cocoa powder is packed with antioxidants and ¾ cup of sweetener keeps the calories down. This has a great chocolate taste, that's also healthy.

Preparation Time About: 5 hours | **Servings:** 3

INGREDIENTS
2 cups water
1 cup unsweetened cocoa powder
3/4 cup agave
2 tablespoons lemon juice
DIRECTIONS
- NOTE: Freeze your ice cream bowl for at least 24hrs prior to starting!
- Mix together the water and agave in a medium saucepan on medium heat. Stir frequently until the agave dissolve. Mix in the cocoa powder and lemon juice and let the mixture come to a simmer. Let the mixture cook for 3 minutes. Allow the mixture to cool completely. Then refrigerate covered for 2 hours.
- Pour the ingredients into your ice cream maker, and let it churn for 25-30 minutes.
- Place in an airtight container for up to 2 hours, until desired consistency is reached.

Soothing Soft Serve Ice Cream

Soft serve ice cream has been around since the stone age and loved by everyone. Taste the deliciousness of something so wonderful as these amazing dessert treats. Turn the pages and pick something you've not tried before. You'll see that you are a fan of something deliciously different!

Nutella & Bananas Soft Serve Ice Cream

As a kid if you ate peanut butter and banana sandwiches you will love this treat! Nutella is a chocolaty hazelnut rich spread that originated in Europe. It pairs well with the texture and sweetness of the bananas. Very delicious indeed!

Preparation Time About: 35 Minutes | **Servings:** 6

INGREDIENTS
1 cup sliced Bananas
6 tbs. Nutella
2 cups heavy cream
1 cup milk
3/4 cup sugar
1 Tbs. vanilla extract
DIRECTIONS
- **NOTE: Freeze your ice cream bowl for at least 24hrs prior to starting!**
- Place the milk and cream in a bowl, and mix them together until well combined. Use a whisk to mix in the sugar. Continue to whisk for about 4 minutes until the sugar dissolves. Then mix in the vanilla extract.
- Place all the ingredients in a food processor or blender, and puree.
- Pour the ingredients into your ice cream maker, and let it churn for 25 minutes.
- Serve immediately.

Peanut Butter White Chocolate Soft Serve Ice cream

This peanut butter chocolate treat adds a lovely richness that combines perfectly with the nutty, creaminess of the peanut butter. This soft serve ice cream is incredibly rich and creamy.

Preparation Time About: 40 Minutes | **Servings:** 6

INGREDIENTS

2 cups heavy cream
1 cup milk
3/4 cup sugar
1 Tbs. vanilla extract
1/2 cup peanut butter slightly melted
2 ounces semi-sweet chocolate

DIRECTIONS

- **NOTE: Freeze your ice cream bowl for at least 24hrs prior to starting!**
- Melt the chocolate in a medium sauce pan on low heat. Allow the chocolate to cool a bit.
- While the chocolate is cooling, place the milk and cream in a bowl, and mix them together until well combined. Use a whisk to mix in the sugar. Continue to whisk for about 4 minutes until the sugar dissolves. Mix in the vanilla extract. Then whisk in the peanut butter, and then the chocolate.
- Pour the ingredients into your ice cream maker, and let it churn for 25 minutes.
- Serve immediately.

Caramel Cookie Crunch Soft Serve Ice Cream

The next time you're at the store, pick up a Twix bars to make your very own soft serve ice cream version of something delicious. It's nice and creamy with caramel and a cookie crunch. You will get lots of ideas from this one.

Preparation Time About: 35 Minutes | **Servings:** 6

INGREDIENTS
2 cups heavy cream
1 cup milk
3/4 cup sugar
1 Tbs. vanilla extract
1 ½ cups chopped mini
1 Twix bar
DIRECTIONS
- NOTE: Freeze your ice cream bowl for at least 24hrs prior to starting!
- Place the milk and cream in a bowl, and mix them together until well combined. Use a whisk to mix in the sugar. Continue to whisk for about 4 minutes until the sugar dissolves. Mix in the vanilla extract.
- Pour the ingredients into your ice cream maker, and let it churn for 25 minutes. About 5 minutes before the ice cream is done churning add the snickers to your ice cream maker.
- Serve immediately.

Rosemary Soft Serve Ice Cream

This soft serve has an interesting aromatic and fresh scented flavor. It maintains a sweetness that balances out the aromatic flavor of the rosemary.

Preparation Time About: 35 Minutes | **Servings:** 6

INGREDIENTS
2 cups heavy cream
1 cup milk
3/4 cup sugar
1 Tbs. vanilla extract
1 ½ cups packed rosemary
DIRECTIONS
- NOTE: Freeze your ice cream bowl for at least 24hrs prior to starting!
- Place the milk and cream in a bowl, and mix them together until well combined. Use a whisk to mix in the sugar. Continue to whisk for about 4 minutes until the sugar dissolves. Mix in the vanilla extract.
- Pulverize the rosemary in a blender or food processor.
- Place all the ingredients in a food processor or blender, and puree.
- Pour the ingredients into your ice cream maker, and let it churn for 25 minutes.
- Serve immediately.

Very Vegan Style Desserts

We always remember to add a special section for the ones watching the healthy scale. You won't believe that some of these delicious flavors are actually some of the healthiest you can make for ice cream desserts. Dive in and savor the flavor.

Basil Chocolate Vegan Soft Serve Ice cream

The chocolate mixed with basil will heighten the pleasures of taste for anyone! This the coconut milk or cream is what makes this soft serve get its creaminess. Very rich but also very fresh with the taste of the mint.

Preparation Time About: 50 Minutes | Cook Time: 10 Minutes | **Servings:** 9

INGREDIENTS

3/4 cup water
1 1/4 cups full fat coconut milk or coconut cream (as thick as possible)
2/3 cup organic cane sugar
2/3 cup unsweetened cocoa powder
1/4 tsp sea salt
6 ounces vegan dark chocolate, finely chopped
1/2 tsp pure vanilla extract
¼ cup basil (pulverized)

DIRECTIONS

- NOTE: Freeze your ice cream bowl for at least 24hrs prior to starting!
- Put the first 5 ingredients in a large saucepan, and heat it on medium-high heat. Mix the ingredients together using a whisk. Allow the mixture to come to a low boil. Continue to whisk often, and remain cooking on a low boil for 1 minute.
- Take the pan off the heat, and mix in the chocolate and vanilla extract using the whisk. Continue to mix until the chocolate is melted then add the basil.
- Place the mixture in a blender, and blend on high speed for about 30 seconds.
- Allow the mixture to cool
- Pour the ingredients into your ice cream maker, and let it churn for 25 minutes.
- Serve immediately.

Blueberry Chocolate Vegan Soft Serve Ice Cream

With this recipe, the blueberry and chocolate blends so well together that you can't fully describe its taste. You just have to experience it. The raspberry gives this ice cream a lovely sweetness that balances out the rich flavor of the chocolate. This ice cream has a deeply rich chocolate flavor.

Preparation Time About: 50 Minutes | Cook Time: 10 Minutes | **Servings:** 9

INGREDIENTS
3/4 cup water
1 1/4 cups full fat coconut milk or coconut cream (as thick as possible)
2/3 cup organic cane sugar
2/3 cup unsweetened cocoa powder
1/4 tsp sea salt
6 ounces vegan dark chocolate, finely chopped
1/2 tsp pure vanilla extract
1/2 cup blueberries

DIRECTIONS
- **NOTE: Freeze your ice cream bowl for at least 24hrs prior to starting!**
- Put the first 5 ingredients in a large saucepan, and heat it on medium-high heat. Mix the ingredients together using a whisk. Allow the mixture to come to a low boil. Continue to whisk often, and remain cooking on a low boil for 1 minute.
- Take the pan off the heat, and mix in the chocolate and vanilla extract using the whisk. Continue to mix until the chocolate is melted.
- Place the mixture in a blender with the blueberries, and blend on high speed for about 30 seconds or until the blueberries are pureed.
- Allow the mixture to cool
- Pour the ingredients into your ice cream maker, and let it churn for 25 minutes.
- Serve immediately.

Cinnamon Soy Vanilla Vegan Soft Serve Ice Cream

You would almost not even know that there is tofu in this ice cream! The coconut milk gives this ice cream a rich texture along with the tofu. Even though this ice cream is vegan, it still has all the great taste of homemade ice cream to anyone who doesn't know.

Preparation Time About: 35 Minutes | **Servings:** Makes 1 Quart

INGREDIENTS
1 pound silken tofu
½ cup plus 2 tablespoons organic or granulated sugar
½ teaspoon kosher salt
1 vanilla bean, split lengthwise
¾ cup refined coconut oil, melted, cooled slightly
2 teaspoons cinnamon

DIRECTIONS
- NOTE: Freeze your ice cream bowl for at least 24hrs prior to starting!
- Put the first 3 ingredients in a blender. Then add in the vanilla bean seeds. Puree the mixture until its smooth, around 15 seconds. Turn the blender to medium speed, and slowly drizzle in the coconut oil and cinnamon. Blend the mixture until its thick, but don't over blend it.
- Pour the ingredients into your ice cream maker, and let it churn for 25 minutes.
- Serve immediately.

Orange Chocolate Almond Vegan Ice cream

This smell of citrus in this Ice cream give you the feeling of feeling good with every spoon full. The almonds give a nice crunch, and a nutty flavor that enhances the chocolate. It has a deep, rich chocolate flavor that matches any traditional ice cream. It is truly heaven in a bowl.

Preparation Time About: 2.5 Hours | **Cook Time:** 10 Minutes | **Servings:** 9

INGREDIENTS
3/4 cup water
1 1/4 cups full fat coconut milk or coconut cream (as thick as possible)
2/3 cup organic cane sugar
2/3 cup unsweetened cocoa powder
1/4 tsp sea salt
6 ounces vegan dark chocolate, finely chopped
1/2 tsp pure vanilla extract
½ cup chopped almonds
½ tsp orange extract

DIRECTIONS
- **NOTE: Freeze your ice cream bowl for at least 24hrs prior to starting!**
- Put the first 5 ingredients in a large saucepan, and heat it on medium-high heat. Mix the ingredients together using a whisk. Allow the mixture to come to a low boil. Continue to whisk often, and remain cooking on a low boil for 1 minute.
- Take the pan off the heat, and mix in the chocolate and vanilla extract using the whisk. Continue to mix until the chocolate is melted.
- Place the mixture in a blender, blend on high (30 seconds) and allow the mixture to cool.
- Pour the ingredients into your ice cream maker, and let it churn for 25 minutes. About 5 minutes before the ice cream is done churning.
- Put the ice cream in an airtight container and place in the freezer for around 2 hours. Allow the ice cream to thaw for 15 minutes before serving.

Pineapple Strawberries N Cream Tofu Vegan Ice Cream

Although it's vegan, this ice cream still has all the great taste of traditional ice cream. By the tofu giving this ice cream a rich texture, along with the coconut milk, you will truly be a lover of this special treat.

Preparation Time About: 35 Minutes | **Servings:** Makes 1 Quart

INGREDIENTS
1 pound silken tofu
½ cup plus 2 tablespoons organic or granulated sugar
½ teaspoon kosher salt
1 vanilla bean, split lengthwise
¾ cup refined coconut oil, melted, cooled slightly
½ cup sliced strawberries
½ cup pineapple
DIRECTIONS
- NOTE: Freeze your ice cream bowl for at least 24hrs prior to starting!
- Put the first 3 ingredients in a blender. Then add in the vanilla bean seeds, pineapples and strawberries. Puree the mixture until its smooth, around 15 seconds. Turn the blender to medium speed, and slowly drizzle in the coconut oil. Blend the mixture until its thick, but don't over blend it.
- Pour the ingredients into your ice cream maker, and let it churn for 25 minutes.
- Put the ice cream in an airtight container and place in the freezer for around 2 hours. Allow the ice cream to thaw for 15 minutes before serving.

Carob Chip Mint Soy Vanilla Vegan Ice Cream

The carob chops are like chocolate, made from the carob tree. The tofu, and coconut milk maintains this ice cream a rich texture together. While it's still vegan, this ice cream still has all the great taste of traditional ice cream. You will love it!

Preparation Time About: 35 Minutes **Servings:** Makes 1 Quart

INGREDIENTS
1 pound silken tofu
½ cup plus 2 tablespoons organic or granulated sugar
½ teaspoon kosher salt
1 vanilla bean, split lengthwise
¾ cup virgin coconut oil, melted, ½ cooled
1 cup vegan carob chips
¼ cup mint (pulverized)
DIRECTIONS
- NOTE: Freeze your ice cream bowl for at least 24hrs prior to starting!
- Put the first 3 ingredients in a blender. Then add in the vanilla bean seeds. Puree the mixture until its smooth, around 15 seconds. Turn the blender to medium speed, and slowly drizzle in the coconut oil. Blend the mixture until its thick, but don't over blend it.
- Pour the ingredients into your ice cream maker, and let it churn for 25 minutes. About 5 minutes before the ice cream is done churning add the carob chips and mint to your ice cream maker.
- Put the ice cream in an airtight container and place in the freezer for around 2 hours. Allow the ice cream to thaw for 15 minutes before serving.

Chocolate Raspberry Pistachio Vegan Gelato

Pistachio, Raspberry and Chocolate...Please give me more! The chocolate adds depth of flavor and a crunchy texture. This gelato is packed with nutty pistachio taste. All I have to say is try this one!

Preparation Time About: 2 Hours 35 Minutes | **Servings:** 4

INGREDIENTS
2 cups shelled, roasted, salted pistachios
1 can coconut milk
1/2 cup arrowroot
¾ cup sugar
1 teaspoon lime juice
4 ounces chopped vegan chocolate
1/4 cup raspberries
DIRECTIONS
* NOTE: Freeze your ice cream bowl for at least 24hrs prior to starting!
* Pulse the pistachios in a food processor for about 3 minutes
* Place all ingredients EXCEPT the chocolate in a blender. Blend on high speed until smooth.
* Pour the mixture into your ice cream maker, and let it churn for 25 minutes. About 5 minutes before the ice cream is done churning add the chocolate to your ice cream maker.
* Put the gelato in an airtight container and place in the freezer for up to 2 hours, until desired consistency is reached.

Lemon Chocolate Blueberry Vegan Gelato

This gelato gets its chocolaty rich flavor from the bananas when they freeze and coconut cream. The strawberries have a sweet bursting taste from the center of the rich chocolate gelato.

Preparation Time About: 2 Hours 35 Minutes | **Servings:** Makes 3 cups

INGREDIENTS
1 ½ cup refrigerated coconut cream
1 cup cut up lemons
3 tablespoons cocoa powder
1/2 teaspoon salt
½ cup blueberries
DIRECTIONS
* NOTE: Freeze your ice cream bowl for at least 24hrs prior to starting!
* Place all ingredients EXCEPT the blueberries in a blender. Blend on high speed until smooth.
* Pour the mixture into your ice cream maker, and let it churn for 25 minutes. About 5 minutes before the ice cream is done churning add the blueberries to your ice cream maker.
* Put the gelato in an airtight container and place in the freezer for up to 2 hours, until desired consistency is reached.

Raspberry Pumpkin Spice Vegan Soy Frozen Yogurt

This raspberry and pumpkin spice is to crave over and over again. It's easy to make frozen yogurt begins with a soy yogurt, then adding the blackberry jam for flavor you won't believe. Use a higher-quality jam for best results.

Preparation Time About: 2 Hours 30 Minutes | **Servings:** 1 Quart

INGREDIENTS
2 ¾ cups unsweetened plain soy yogurt
1¼ raspberry jam
1 tbsp. pumpkin spice
DIRECTIONS
- NOTE: Freeze your ice cream bowl for at least 24hrs prior to starting!
- Place the yogurt in a bowl and mix in the jam. Use a hand mixer to beat the mixture for 5 minutes.
- Pour the ingredients into your ice cream maker, and let it churn for 25 minutes.
- Put the frozen yogurt in an airtight container and place in the freezer for at least 2 hours, until desired consistency is reached.

Blackberry Lemon Coconut Vegan Frozen Yogurt

Keep it coming with the tartness of the blackberries and lemons, but it is also tamed down with the sweetness of the maple syrup. This frozen yogurt is married with the succulent sweet taste of the tropical rich flavor of coconut. Try topping this one with vegan chocolate sauce. Wow!!!

Preparation Time About: 2 Hours 35 Minutes | **Servings:** 1 Quart

INGREDIENTS
2 cups coconut yogurt
1/4 cup sugar or maple syrup
1/2 teaspoon vanilla extract
1/4 cup shredded coconut
½ cup blackberries
1 lemon
DIRECTIONS
- NOTE: Freeze your ice cream bowl for at least 24hrs prior to starting!
- Puree the blackberries and lemon in a food processor or blender.
- Place the yogurt in a bowl. Use a whisk to mix in the sugar. Continue to whisk for about 4 minutes until the sugar dissolves. Then mix in the vanilla extract, and blackberry puree.
- Pour the ingredients into your ice cream maker, and let it churn for 25 minutes. About 5 minutes before the ice cream is done churning add the shredded coconut to your ice cream maker.
- Put the frozen yogurt in an airtight container and place in the freezer for at least 2 hours, until desired consistency is reached.

Chocolate Cherry Cocoa Banana Vegan Milkshake

You had me at chocolate, cherry banana! The taste of creamy chocolate covered banana with cherries is got a good balance of a rich succulent flavor you will savor for hours after it's gone.

Preparation Time About: 40 Minutes | Cook Time: 10 Minutes | **Servings:** 9

INGREDIENTS

3/4 cup water
1 1/4 cups full fat coconut milk or coconut cream (as thick as possible)
2/3 cup organic cane sugar
2/3 cup unsweetened cocoa powder
1/4 tsp sea salt
6 oz. vegan dark chocolate, finely chopped
1/2 tsp pure vanilla extract
¼ cup sliced frozen bananas
¼ cup cherries (cut up fine)
1 tbsp. cinnamon

DIRECTIONS

- NOTE: Freeze your ice cream bowl for at least 24hrs prior to starting!
- Put the first 5 ingredients in a large saucepan, and heat it on medium-high heat. Mix the ingredients together using a whisk. Allow the mixture to come to a low boil. Continue to whisk often, and remain cooking on a low boil for 1 minute.
- Take the pan off the heat, and mix in the chocolate and vanilla extract using the whisk. Continue to mix until the chocolate is melted. Add cherries and cinnamon.
- Place the mixture in a blender with the bananas, and blend on high speed for about 30 seconds, then allow the mixture to cool
- Pour the ingredients into your ice cream maker, and let it churn for 10-15 minutes, until desired consistency is reached and serve immediately.

Chocolate Peppermint Banana Vegan Milkshake

Any way you look at it, mint and chocolate go so well together. But add the bananas and this one will blow your mind! Fresh mint goes with the rich complex flavor of the chocolate and the peppermint is the icing on the cake! Enjoy!

Preparation Time About: 40 Minutes | Cook Time: 10 Minutes | **Servings:** 9

INGREDIENTS

3/4 cup water
1 1/4 cups full fat coconut milk or coconut cream (as thick as possible)
2/3 cup organic cane sugar
2/3 cup unsweetened cocoa powder
1/4 tsp sea salt
6 ounces vegan dark chocolate, finely chopped
11/2 tsp peppermint extract
½ cup sliced frozen bananas

DIRECTIONS

- NOTE: Freeze your ice cream bowl for at least 24hrs prior to starting!
- Put the first 5 ingredients in a large saucepan, and heat it on medium-high heat. Mix the ingredients together using a whisk. Allow the mixture to come to a low boil. Continue to whisk often, and remain cooking on a low boil for 1 minute.
- Take the pan off the heat, and mix in the chocolate and mint extract using the whisk. Continue to mix until the chocolate is melted.
- Place mixture in a blender with the bananas, and blend on high speed for about 30 seconds.
- Allow the mixture to cool
- Pour the ingredients into your ice cream maker, and let it churn for 10-15 minutes, until desired consistency is reached.
- Serve immediately.

Fun Stuff for the Kiddos

The kids will just love this section that we've prepared for you. The pleasures of ice cream just elevated to the next level. Kids, get ready to help your parent make some of the most flavorful ice creams on the planet! We've done this one just for you! Enjoy! ;)

Orange Cola Soft Serve Ice Cream

Mixing orange and cola at the fountain machine when we were younger was so much fun! So, we've made something special just for you! This one should make some smiles last longer, for sure!

Preparation Time About: 55 Minutes | **Servings:** 6

INGREDIENTS
2 cups heavy cream
1 cup milk
3/4 cup sugar
1 tbsp. orange extract
1 tbs. vanilla extract
3 cups coca cola (2, 12 ounce cans)

DIRECTIONS
- **NOTE: Freeze your ice cream bowl for at least 24hrs prior to starting!**
- Pour the coke into a large skillet, and heat it on high heat until it comes to a boil. Allow the coke to cook for about another 15 or 20 minutes, until the coke reduces down to 1 cup of liquid. Let the liquid cool.
- Place the milk and cream in a bowl, and mix them together until well combined. Use a whisk to mix in the sugar. Continue to whisk for about 4 minutes until the sugar dissolves. Mix in the vanilla and orange extract, then the coca cola.
- Pour the ingredients into your ice cream maker, and let it churn for 25 minutes.
- Serve immediately.

Bubble Gum Cola Soft Serve Ice Cream

Well you know that the kids love the flavor of bubble gum, so adding it to this special soft serve ice cream will be a treat.

Preparation Time About: 35 Minutes | **Servings:** 6

INGREDIENTS
2 cups heavy cream
1 cup milk
3/4 cup sugar
1 Tbs. vanilla extract
1 gram bubble gum flavoring
½ cup mini gum balls
½ cup coca cola
DIRECTIONS
- NOTE: Freeze your ice cream bowl for at least 24hrs prior to starting!
- Place the milk and cream in a bowl, and mix them together until well combined. Use a whisk to mix in the sugar. Continue to whisk for about 4 minutes until the sugar dissolves. Mix in the vanilla extract, coca cola and then the bubble gum flavoring.
- Pour the ingredients into your ice cream maker, and let it churn for 25 minutes. About 5 minutes before the churning is done add the gum balls to your ice cream maker.
- Serve immediately.

Blueberry Honey Cake Batter Soft Serve Ice Cream

By adding cake batter in this flavorful ice cream will really have this dessert taste just like real cake. Think of this one for any occasion for your kids, especially for a birthday party!

Preparation Time About: 35 Minutes | **Servings:** 6

INGREDIENTS
2 cups heavy cream
1 cup milk
3/4 cup sugar
1 Tbs. vanilla extract
2/3 cup cake mix
½ cup blueberries
2 tablespoons honey
DIRECTIONS
- NOTE: Freeze your ice cream bowl for at least 24hrs prior to starting!
- Place the milk and cream in a bowl, and mix them together until well combined. Use a whisk to mix in the sugar. Continue to whisk for about 4 minutes until the sugar dissolves. Mix in the vanilla extract, and then the 2/3 cup cake mix honey and blueberries.
- Pour the ingredients into your ice cream maker, and let it churn for 25 minutes.
- Serve immediately.

Butter Toffee Popcorn Soft Serve Ice Cream

Hey kids, popcorn is on the menu, and we've added it to your ice cream! This one has a very interesting texture and with the butter toffee involved, you are sure to hit a home run with this one.

Preparation Time About: 35 Minutes | **Servings:** 6

INGREDIENTS
2 cups heavy cream
1 cup milk
3/4 cup sugar
1 Tbs. vanilla extract
2 cup butter toffee popcorn
DIRECTIONS
- NOTE: Freeze your ice cream bowl for at least 24hrs prior to starting!
- Place the milk and cream in a bowl, and mix them together until well combined. Use a whisk to mix in the sugar. Continue to whisk for about 4 minutes until the sugar dissolves. Mix in the vanilla extract. Place the mixture in a blender or food processor with 1 cup of the caramel corn, and puree.
- Put the remaining caramel corn in a resealable plastic bag, and seal it. Crush the caramel corn using your hands, or a mallet.
- Pour the ingredients into your ice cream maker, and let it churn for 25 minutes. About 5 minutes before the churning is finished add in the crushed caramel corn.
- Serve immediately.

Gummy Worm Cotton Candy Ice Cream

You will feel like you are at the amusement park when you pull this one out of your playbook. Make sure you invite all of your kid's friends over for a treat they will love you for. Oh, by the way, the gummies are like the additional frosting on the cake. They won't believe you made it!

Preparation Time About: 2 Hours 50 Minutes | **Servings:** 6

INGREDIENTS
2 cups heavy cream
1 cup milk
3/4 cup sugar
1 tablespoon vanilla extract
1 tablespoon cotton candy extract
1 ½ cups gummy worm candy
DIRECTIONS
- NOTE: Freeze your ice cream bowl for at least 24hrs prior to starting!
- Place the milk and cream in a bowl, and mix them together until well combined. Use a whisk to mix in the sugar. Continue to whisk for about 4 minutes until the sugar dissolves. Then mix in the vanilla extract.
- Pour the ingredients into your ice cream maker, and let it churn for 25 minutes. About 5 minutes before the ice cream is done churning add the M&Ms to your ice cream maker.
- Put the ice cream in an airtight container and place in the freezer for around 2 hours. Allow the ice cream to thaw for 15 minutes before serving.

Sour Patch Chocolate Ice Cream

If your kiddos like it sour and tart then this one is a special treat. Make sure they've been good before you serve this one up. The yummy taste of chocolate with the sour patch will make them scream for more. Enjoy!

Preparation Time About: 2 Hours 50 Minutes | **Servings:** 6

INGREDIENTS
2 cups heavy cream
1 cup milk
3/4 cup sugar
1 tablespoon vanilla extract
1 cups chopped sour patch
½ cup chocolate (chopped fine)
DIRECTIONS
- NOTE: Freeze your ice cream bowl for at least 24hrs prior to starting!
- Place the milk and cream in a bowl, and mix them together until well combined. Use a whisk to mix in the sugar. Continue to whisk for about 4 minutes until the sugar dissolves. Then mix in the vanilla extract.
- Pour the ingredients into your ice cream maker, and let it churn for 25 minutes. About 5 minutes before the ice cream is done churning add the sour patch and chocolate to your ice cream maker.
- Put the ice cream in an airtight container and place in the freezer for around 2 hours. Allow the ice cream to thaw for 15 minutes before serving.

Dr. Pepper Cherry Lime Ice Cream

Cherry lime mixed in the wonderful taste of Dr. Pepper...believe it to be true! This flavorful treat will be an amazing ice cream Sunday. Don't forget the whipped cream with cherries.

Preparation Time About: 2 Hours 50 Minutes | **Servings:** 6

INGREDIENTS
2 cups heavy cream
1 cup milk
3/4 cup sugar
1 tablespoon vanilla extract
3 cups (2, 12 ounce cans) Dr. Pepper
½ cup mashed up cherries
1 tablespoon lime juice
DIRECTIONS
- NOTE: Freeze your ice cream bowl for at least 24hrs prior to starting!
- Pour the dr. pepper into a large skillet, and heat it on high heat until it comes to a boil. Allow the coke to cook for about another 15 or 20 minutes, until the root beer reduces down to 1 cup of liquid. Let the liquid cool.
- Place the milk and cream in a bowl, and mix them together until well combined. Use a whisk to mix in the sugar. Continue to whisk for about 4 minutes until the sugar dissolves. Then mix in the vanilla extract, lime juice Dr. pepper reduction and cherries.
- Pour the ingredients into your ice cream maker, and let it churn for 25 minutes. \
- Put the ice cream in an airtight container and place in the freezer for around 2 hours. Allow the ice cream to thaw for 15 minutes before serving.

Classic Root Beer Lemon Gelato

A root beer float is something that everyone craves on any occasion. But to make a gelato by adding the wonderful taste of lemon to enhance the flavor of the root beer is one trick you must try immediately. It's so delicious, but make sure you same some for the kids. ;)

Preparation Time About: 2 Hours 50 Minutes | **Servings:** 4-6

INGREDIENTS
1/2 cup heavy cream
2 cups milk
3/4 cup sugar
1 teaspoon vanilla extract
3 cups (2, 12 ounce cans) root beer
2 tablespoons lemon juice
DIRECTIONS
- **NOTE: Freeze your ice cream bowl for at least 24hrs prior to starting!**
- Pour the root beer into a large skillet, and heat it on high heat until it comes to a boil. Allow the coke to cook for about another 15 or 20 minutes, until the root beer reduces down to 1 cup of liquid. Let the liquid cool.
- Place the milk and cream in a bowl, and mix them together until well combined. Use a whisk to mix in the sugar. Continue to whisk for about 4 minutes until the sugar dissolves. Then mix in the vanilla extract and root beer reduction and lemon juice.
- Pour the ingredients into your ice cream maker, and let it churn for 25 minutes. About 5 minutes before the ice cream is done churning add the chocolate to your ice cream maker.
- Put the gelato in an airtight container and place in the freezer for up to 2 hours, until desired consistency is reached.

Green Apple Musketeer Gelato

Green apple and a musketeer is something we ran across when playing with some of these delicious flavors. You know what they say, "Don't knock it till you try it."

Preparation Time About: 2 Hours 35 Minutes | **Servings:** 4-6

INGREDIENTS
1/2 cup heavy cream
2 cups milk
3/4 cup sugar
1 tablespoon vanilla extract
1 ½ cups chopped mini Musketeers bars
¼ cup green apples
DIRECTIONS
- **NOTE: Freeze your ice cream bowl for at least 24hrs prior to starting!**
- Place the milk and cream in a bowl, and mix them together until well combined. Use a whisk to mix in the sugar. Continue to whisk for about 4 minutes until the sugar dissolves. Then mix in the vanilla extract.
- Pour the ingredients into your ice cream maker, and let it churn for 25 minutes. About 5 minutes before the ice cream is done churning add the three musketeers and green apples to your ice cream maker.
- Put the gelato in an airtight container and place in the freezer for up to 2 hours, until desired consistency is reached.

Butterfinger Cinnamon Crunch Gelato

The cinnamon buttery crunch gelato. One of our all-time favorites and we are sure your kids will say the same. No need to say anymore with this one.

Preparation Time About: 2 Hours 35 Minutes | **Servings:** 4-6

INGREDIENTS

1/2 cup heavy cream
2 cups milk
3/4 cup sugar
1 teaspoon vanilla extract
1 ½ cups chopped mini Butterfinger bars
2 teaspoons ground cinnamon

DIRECTIONS

- NOTE: Freeze your ice cream bowl for at least 24hrs prior to starting!
- Place the milk and cream in a bowl, and mix them together until well combined. Use a whisk to mix in the sugar. Continue to whisk for about 4 minutes until the sugar dissolves. Then mix in the vanilla extract and cinnamon.
- Pour the ingredients into your ice cream maker, and let it churn for 25 minutes. About 5 minutes before the ice cream is done churning add the Butterfinger to your ice cream maker.
- Put the gelato in an airtight container and place in the freezer for up to 2 hours, until desired consistency is reached.

S'mores Camp Fire Frozen Yogurt

Nothing will make your kids say "Yummm" like making S'mores by a campfire. Well, you don't need to do all of that when you can play, "I'm changing up the dessert to ice cream." For professional moms, stick a piece of graham cracker in the bowl.

Preparation Time About: 2 Hours 35 Minutes | **Servings:** 1 Quart

INGREDIENTS
1 quart container full-fat plain yogurt
¼ teaspoon salt
1 cup sugar
1 teaspoon vanilla extract
3 large graham crackers
4 ounces chopped semi-sweet chocolate
½ cup mini marshmallows
1 tsp smoke flavor extract

DIRECTIONS
- **NOTE: Freeze your ice cream bowl for at least 24hrs prior to starting!**
- Place the yogurt in a bowl. Use a whisk to mix in the sugar and salt. Continue to whisk for about 4 minutes until the sugar dissolves. Then mix in the vanilla and smoke flavored extract.
- Place the graham crackers in a food processor, and process until the crackers are no bigger than chocolate chips. If you don't have a food processor place the crackers in a large resealable plastic bag, and seal it shut. Use your hands, a mallet, or a rolling pin to crush the cookies.
- Pour the ingredients into your ice cream maker, and let it churn for 25 minutes. About 5 minutes before the ice cream is done churning add the chocolate, graham crackers, and marshmallows to your ice cream maker.
- Put the frozen yogurt in an airtight container and place in the freezer for at least 2 hours, until desired consistency is reached.

Cherry Blueberry Lime Soda Frozen Yogurt

We're adding an array of delicious twisted flavors that will have those kiddo's running back for more. All inside of this flavorful frozen yogurt for anyone to indulge!

Preparation Time About: 2 Hours 50 Minutes | **Servings:** 1 Quart

INGREDIENTS
1 quart container full-fat plain yogurt
¼ teaspoon salt
1 cup sugar
½ lime (peeled and cut up fine)
1/2 cup blueberries
1 teaspoon vanilla extract
3 cups (2, 12 ounce cans) cherry soda

DIRECTIONS
- NOTE: Freeze your ice cream bowl for at least 24hrs prior to starting!
- Pour the cherry soda into a large skillet, and heat it on high heat until it comes to a boil. Allow the coke to cook for about another 15 or 20 minutes, until the root beer reduces down to 1 cup of liquid. Let the liquid cool.
- Place the yogurt in a bowl. Use a whisk to mix in the sugar and salt. Continue to whisk for about 4 minutes until the sugar dissolves. Then mix in the vanilla extract, blueberries, lime and reduced cherry soda.
- Pour the ingredients into your ice cream maker, and let it churn for 25 minutes.
- Put the frozen yogurt in an airtight container and place in the freezer for at least 2 hours, until desired consistency is reached.

Chocolate Cookie Rice Crispy Treat Frozen Yogurt

This "Fro Yo" version of chocolate with the texture of Rice crispy treats are always a hit in any home. Adding the chocolate enhances the rich creamy texture even more. Parents...you better save some for the kids!

Preparation Time About: 2 Hours 35 Minutes	**Servings:** 1 Quart

INGREDIENTS

1 quart container full-fat plain yogurt
¼ teaspoon salt
1 cup sugar
1 teaspoon vanilla extract
10 chocolate sandwich cookies
1/2 cup rice crispy treats
¼ cup milk chocolate (chopped fine)

DIRECTIONS

- NOTE: Freeze your ice cream bowl for at least 24hrs prior to starting!
- Place the yogurt in a bowl. Use a whisk to mix in the sugar and salt. Continue to whisk for about 4 minutes until the sugar dissolves. Then mix in the vanilla extract.
- Place the sandwich cookies in a food processor, and process until the cookies are no bigger than chocolate chips. If you don't have a food processor place the cookies in a large resealable plastic bag, and seal it shut. Use your hands, a mallet, or a rolling pin to crush the cookies.
- Pour the ingredients into your ice cream maker, and let it churn for 25 minutes. About 5 minutes before the ice cream is done churning add the cookies, and small chunks of the rice crispy treats to your ice cream maker.
- Put the frozen yogurt in an airtight container and place in the freezer for at least 2 hours, until desired consistency is reached.

Red Velvet Raspberry Milkshake

Oooh, the flavor of red velvet cake is yummy and delicious. Mixing in the raspberry gives this one an unbelievable flavor you won't believe! A treat indeed and something to savor for days!

Preparation Time About: 25 Minutes | **Servings:** 6

INGREDIENTS
2 cups heavy cream
1 cup milk
3/4 cup sugar
1 teaspoons vanilla extract
1 - 8-ounce package cream cheese, softened
1 tablespoon cocoa powder
1 tablespoon & 1 teaspoon red food coloring
¼ cup raspberries
DIRECTIONS
- NOTE: Freeze your ice cream bowl for at least 24hrs prior to starting!
- Place the milk and cream in a bowl, and mix them together until well combined. Use a whisk to mix in the sugar. Continue to whisk for about 4 minutes until the sugar dissolves. Put all the ingredients in a blender and pulse for around 30 seconds until well mixed.
- Pour the ingredients into your ice cream maker, and let it churn for 10-15 minutes, until desired consistency is reached.
- Serve immediately.

Graham Cracker Peanut Butter Cup Milkshake

This graham cracker delight is a must try in the home of anyone who likes peanut butter. The chocolate makes it even better and all in the form of a milkshake. Trust me...when it's all gone, mom will make more!

Preparation Time About: 25 Minutes | **Servings:** 6

INGREDIENTS
2 cups heavy cream
1 cup milk
3/4 cup sugar
1 tablespoon vanilla extract
1 1/2 cups chopped mini peanut butter cups
½ cup maple syrup
4 graham crackers
DIRECTIONS
- NOTE: Freeze your ice cream bowl for at least 24hrs prior to starting!
- Place the milk and cream in a bowl, and mix them together until well combined. Use a whisk to mix in the sugar. Continue to whisk for about 4 minutes until the sugar dissolves. Then mix in the vanilla extract.
- Pour the ingredients into your ice cream maker, and let it churn for 10-15 minutes, until desired consistency is reached. About 5 minutes before the ice cream is done churning add the peanut butter cup and the graham crackers to your ice cream maker.
- Serve immediately.

Circus Cotton Candy Milkshake

No need to go to the circus for this milkshake treat. Enhancing the flavors of a milkshake can create a craving in your home that will be unbelievable. This sweet, succulent and amazing milkshake is simple, but in our top 10 flavors in this book!

Preparation Time About: 25 Minutes | **Servings:** 6

INGREDIENTS
2 cups heavy cream
1 cup milk
3/4 cup sugar
1 teaspoon vanilla extract
1/2 cup cotton candy syrup
1 tablespoon plus 1 teaspoon pink or blue food coloring
DIRECTIONS
- NOTE: Freeze your ice cream bowl for at least 24hrs prior to starting!
- Place the milk and cream in a bowl, and mix them together until well combined. Use a whisk to mix in the sugar. Continue to whisk for about 4 minutes until the sugar dissolves. Then mix in the vanilla extract, syrup, and food coloring.
- Pour the ingredients into your ice cream maker, and let it churn for 10-15 minutes, until desired consistency is reached.
- Serve immediately.

Tropical Coconut Banana Animal Cracker Sorbet

It's never too late for animal crackers. This is a sorbet, well worth waiting for. Having this tropical twist of flavors pairs well after any meal when the kids have been good! Let them help you with this one, but make sure they don't eat all of the animal crackers. They'll want to scoop them in their sorbet.

Preparation Time About: 2 hours 40 Minutes | **Servings:** 4-8

INGREDIENTS
3 peeled, mashed bananas
2-4 tablespoons honey to taste
1 1/2 cups light coconut milk
1 teaspoon vanilla extract
10 animal crackers
DIRECTIONS
- NOTE: Freeze your ice cream bowl for at least 24hrs prior to starting!
- Puree all ingredients in a food processor or blender. Taste, and add more honey if desired.
- Pour the ingredients into your ice cream maker, and let it churn for 25-30 minutes. Mix in the animal crackers about 5 minutes before sorbet is complete.
- Place in an airtight container for up to 2 hours, until desired consistency is reached.

Adult Bonus Section!

We always say that the adults need to play too! This is our bonus section for all of the adults out there who work so hard and need a break for the world. You will find that making ice cream is great, but to add a little something that kicks in the flavors of the ice cream is just a special treat!

Chocolate Screwdriver Soft Serve Ice Cream

After a long, hard day of work, kick your feet up, go to the freezer and pull out some of this delicious dessert. By adding chocolate to this screwdriver soft serve you'll know just what we're saying!

Preparation Time About: 35 Minutes | **Servings:** 6

INGREDIENTS
2 cups heavy cream
1 cup milk
3/4 cup sugar
1 Tbs. vanilla extract
1 tbsp. coco powder
½ cup orange juice
3 tablespoons vodka

DIRECTIONS
- NOTE: Freeze your ice cream bowl for at least 24hrs prior to starting!
- Place the milk and cream in a bowl, and mix them together until well combined. Use a whisk to mix in the sugar. Continue to whisk for about 4 minutes until the sugar dissolves. Mix in the vanilla extract and coco powder. Then mix in the orange juice. Finally whisk in the vodka.
- Pour the ingredients into your ice cream maker, and let it churn for 25 minutes.
- Serve immediately.

Grown Folks "Old Fashioned" Ice Cream

After making this one you'll see that this one taste just like the real thing. However, added to ice cream takes it to a level beyond your wildest dreams.

Preparation Time About: 2 Hours 50 Minutes | **Servings:** 6

INGREDIENTS
2 cups heavy cream
1 cup milk
3/4 cup sugar
1 tablespoon vanilla extract
3 tablespoons whiskey
1 dash of bitters

DIRECTIONS
- NOTE: Freeze your ice cream bowl for at least 24hrs prior to starting!
- Place the milk and cream in a bowl, and mix them together until well combined. Use a whisk to mix in the sugar. Continue to whisk for about 4 minutes until the sugar dissolves. Then mix in the vanilla extract, whiskey, and bitters.
- Pour the ingredients into your ice cream maker, and let it churn for 25 minutes.
- Put the ice cream in an airtight container and place in the freezer for around 2 hours. Allow the ice cream to thaw for 15 minutes before serving.

The Original "Manhattan" Ice Cream

You deserve a break today with some of the delicious flavors of whiskey, vermouth, and bitters. A genuine Manhattan indeed. Indulge and enjoy!

Preparation Time About: 2 Hours 50 Minutes | **Servings:** 6

INGREDIENTS
2 cups heavy cream
1 cup milk
3/4 cup sugar
1 tablespoon vanilla extract
3 tablespoons whiskey
1 tablespoon vermouth
1 dash of bitters

DIRECTIONS
- NOTE: Freeze your ice cream bowl for at least 24hrs prior to starting!
- Place the milk and cream in a bowl, and mix them together until well combined. Use a whisk to mix in the sugar. Continue to whisk for about 4 minutes until the sugar dissolves. Then mix in the vanilla extract, whiskey, vermouth, and bitters.
- Pour the ingredients into your ice cream maker, and let it churn for 25 minutes.
- Put the ice cream in an airtight container and place in the freezer for around 2 hours. Allow the ice cream to thaw for 15 minutes before serving.

Kahlua & Pistachio Ice Cream

Save this one for when you have your friends around. If you have a sweet tooth and love coffee, this ice cream is for you. The sweet coffee almond flavor of Kahlua with the pistachios blends a very interesting delicious flavor to this ice cream treat.

Preparation Time About: 2 Hours 50 Minutes | **Servings:** 6

INGREDIENTS
2 cups heavy cream
1 cup milk
3/4 cup sugar
1 teaspoon vanilla extract
3 tablespoons Kahlua
3/4 cup chops almond

DIRECTIONS
- NOTE: Freeze your ice cream bowl for at least 24hrs prior to starting!
- Place the milk and cream in a bowl, and mix them together until well combined. Use a whisk to mix in the sugar. Continue to whisk for about 4 minutes until the sugar dissolves. Then mix in the vanilla extract, Kahlua.
- Pour the ingredients into your ice cream maker, and let it churn for 25 minutes. About 5 minutes before the ice cream is done churning add the almonds to your ice cream maker.
- Put the ice cream in an airtight container and place in the freezer for around 2 hours. Allow the ice cream to thaw for 15 minutes before serving.

Tropical Watermelon Lemon/Lime Sorbet

This is a very refreshing taste of sorbet and will go over well with that special friend or loved one. Make sure they help you in the kitchen when preparing this one. They just won't believe that you made it yourself.

Preparation Time About: 2 hours 40 Minutes | **Servings:** Makes 1 Quart

INGREDIENTS
3 1/2 cups sliced seedless watermelon
6-ounce chilled pineapple juice
3/4 cup chilled ginger ale
½ cup fresh lime juice
1/3 cup grenadine
DIRECTIONS
- NOTE: Freeze your ice cream bowl for at least 24hrs prior to starting!
- Puree all ingredients in a food processor or blender.
- Pour the ingredients into your ice cream maker, and let it churn for 25-30 minutes.
- Place in an airtight container for up to 2 hours, until desired consistency is reached.

Strawberry Cinnamon Margarita Soft Serve Ice Cream

Margaritas are a special favorite of most, however in a soft serve ice cream it's just down right delicious. You may never have a margarita without ice cream again! The cinnamon gives this one just what it needs to complete the process.

Preparation Time About: 35 Minutes | **Servings:** 6

INGREDIENTS
2 cups heavy cream
1 cup milk
3/4 cup sugar
1 Tbs. vanilla extract
3 tablespoons tequila
1 tablespoon cinnamon
1/2 cup lime juice
¼ cup strawberries (mashed up)
2 tablespoons orange liqueur
DIRECTIONS
- NOTE: Freeze your ice cream bowl for at least 24hrs prior to starting!
- Place the milk and cream in a bowl, and mix them together until well combined. Use a whisk to mix in the sugar and cinnamon. Continue to whisk for about 4 minutes until the sugar dissolves. Mix the vanilla extract and whisk in the lime juice, strawberries, tequila, and liqueur.
- Pour the ingredients into your ice cream maker, and let it churn for 25 minutes.
- Serve immediately.

Orange Tequila "Sunrise" Gelato

This is the perfect gelato when you want something sweet and boozy. The grenadine gives this ice cream a nice fruity taste along with the orange juice to kick in the flavor. Well of course the tequila provides nice added wildness to this gelato.

Preparation Time About: 2 Hours 35 Minutes | **Servings:** 4-6

INGREDIENTS
1/2 cup heavy cream
2 cups milk
3/4 cup sugar
1/2 cup orange juice
1 teaspoon vanilla extract
3 tablespoons tequila
½ tablespoon grenadine

DIRECTIONS
- NOTE: Freeze your ice cream bowl for at least 24hrs prior to starting!
- Place the milk and cream in a bowl, and mix them together until well combined. Use a whisk to mix in the sugar. Continue to whisk for about 4 minutes until the sugar dissolves. Then mix in the vanilla extract, orange juice, tequila and grenadine.
- Pour the ingredients into your ice cream maker, and let it churn for 25 minutes.
- Put the gelato in an airtight container and place in the freezer for up to 2 hours, until desired consistency is reached.

Mango Strawberry Mint Daiquiri Milkshake

Let's think about this one...Mango, strawberries and mint. Love the combination! When you add the creaminess of the ice cream, you will have a new love of something special to add to your dessert playbook! This one is a winner indeed!

Preparation Time About: 25 Minutes | **Servings:** 6

INGREDIENTS
2 cups heavy cream
1 cup milk
3/4 cup sugar
8 ounces strawberries
¼ cup mint
¼ cup mango
4 tablespoons rum

DIRECTIONS
- NOTE: Freeze your ice cream bowl for at least 24hrs prior to starting!
- Puree the strawberries, mango and mint in a food processor or blender.
- Place the milk and cream in a bowl, and mix them together until well combined. Use a whisk to mix in the sugar. Continue to whisk for about 4 minutes until the sugar dissolves. Then mix in the rum, and strawberry puree.
- Pour the ingredients into your ice cream maker, and let it churn for 10-15 minutes, until desired consistency is reached. About 5 minutes before the ice cream is done churning add the peanut butter cup to your ice cream maker.
- Serve immediately.

Lemon Tequila "Sunset" Gelato

This is the perfect gelato when you want something sweet and boozy. The orange juice and grenadine give this ice cream a nice fruity taste, and the tequila provides a kick.

Preparation Time About: 2 Hours 35 Minutes | **Servings:** 4-6

INGREDIENTS

1/2 cup heavy cream
2 cups milk
3/4 cup sugar
I/2 cup lemon juice
1 teaspoon vanilla extract
3 tablespoons tequila
½ tablespoon grenadine

DIRECTIONS

- NOTE: Freeze your ice cream bowl for at least 24hrs prior to starting!
- Place the milk and cream in a bowl, and mix them together until well combined. Use a whisk to mix in the sugar. Continue to whisk for about 4 minutes until the sugar dissolves. Then mix in the vanilla extract, lemon juice, tequila and grenadine.
- Pour the ingredients into your ice cream maker, and let it churn for 25 minutes.
- Put the gelato in an airtight container and place in the freezer for up to 2 hours, until desired consistency is reached.

Tropical Coconut Rum and Coke Gelato

Now you can enjoy this sweet alcoholic beverage in a creamy frozen form. This gelato won't get you tipsy, but it will have you feeling good.

Preparation Time About: 2 Hours 50 Minutes | **Servings:** 4-6

INGREDIENTS

1/2 cup heavy cream
2 cups milk
3/4 cup sugar
1 teaspoon vanilla extract
3 tablespoons rum
¼ cup shaved coconut
3 cups coca cola (2, 12 ounce cans)

DIRECTIONS

- NOTE: Freeze your ice cream bowl for at least 24hrs prior to starting!
- Pour the coke into a large skillet, and heat it on high heat until it comes to a boil. Allow the coke to cook for about another 15 or 20 minutes, until the coke reduces down to 1 cup of liquid. Let the liquid cool.
- Place the milk and cream in a bowl, and mix them together until well combined. Use a whisk to mix in the sugar. Continue to whisk for about 4 minutes until the sugar dissolves. Then mix in the vanilla extract, coke reduction, coconut chips and rum.
- Pour the ingredients into your ice cream maker, and let it churn for 25 minutes.
- Put the gelato in an airtight container and place in the freezer for up to 2 hours, until desired consistency is reached.

Caribbean Colada Frozen Yogurt

No need to go on vacation to that perfect tropical island for this Colada. You can have this from the comfort of your very own home. Yummy, delicious and just the right amount of rum to enhance the colada flavor.

Preparation Time About: 2 Hours 35 Minutes | **Servings:** 1 Quart

INGREDIENTS
1 quart container full-fat plain yogurt
¼ teaspoon salt
1 cup sugar
½ cup pineapple juice
1 drop coconut essence
2 teaspoons lime juice
1/4 cup shredded coconut
4 tablespoons rum
DIRECTIONS
- NOTE: Freeze your ice cream bowl for at least 24hrs prior to starting!
- Place the yogurt in a bowl. Use a whisk to mix in the sugar and salt. Continue to whisk for about 4 minutes until the sugar dissolves. Then mix in the rum, pineapple juice, lime juice, and coconut essence.
- Pour the ingredients into your ice cream maker, and let it churn for 25 minutes. About 5 minutes before the ice cream is done churning add the shredded coconut to your ice cream maker.
- Put the frozen yogurt in an airtight container and place in the freezer for at least 2 hours, until desired consistency is reached.

Daiquiri Lime Soda Frozen Yogurt

You may not think of soda to go along with a daiquiri but when you get a taste of this frozen yogurt treat, you will become a lover of soda daiquiri's. Creamy sweet texture, lime and soda.

Preparation Time About: 2 Hours 35 Minutes | **Servings:** 1 Quart

INGREDIENTS
1 quart container full-fat plain yogurt
¼ teaspoon salt
1 cup sugar
1/4 cup lime juice
¼ cup sprite
4 tablespoons rum
DIRECTIONS
- NOTE: Freeze your ice cream bowl for at least 24hrs prior to starting!
- Place the yogurt in a bowl. Use a whisk to mix in the sugar and salt. Continue to whisk for about 4 minutes until the sugar dissolves. Then mix in the rum, and lime juice.
- Pour the ingredients into your ice cream maker, and let it churn for 25 minutes.
- Put the frozen yogurt in an airtight container and place in the freezer for at least 2 hours, until desired consistency is reached.

"The Big Stout" Almond Chocolate Milkshake

For all your stout beer lovers out there, this is for you! The stout beer has a nice rich flavor that pairs very well with the semi-sweet chocolate. It's super delicious, even if you are not a beer lover!

Preparation Time About: 25 Minutes | **Servings:** 6

INGREDIENTS
2 cups heavy cream
1 cup milk
3/4 cup sugar
4 ounces chopped semi-sweet chocolate
3 tablespoons almonds
3 tablespoons Guinness beer
DIRECTIONS
- NOTE: Freeze your ice cream bowl for at least 24hrs prior to starting!
- Melt the chocolate, and let it cool for a bit.
- Place the milk and cream in a bowl, and mix them together until well combined. Use a whisk to mix in the sugar. Continue to whisk for about 4 minutes until the sugar dissolves. Then mix in the chocolate and Guinness.
- Pour the ingredients into your ice cream maker, and let it churn for 10-15 minutes, until desired consistency is reached. About 5 minutes before the ice cream is done churning add the almonds to your ice cream maker.
- Serve immediately.

Double Gin and Juice Vanilla Soft Serve Ice Cream

Now you're if you've never had gin this one will make you a lover of the soft serve ice cream world. It's creamy, it's delicious with just a hint of something special. Enjoy!

Preparation Time About: 35 Minutes | **Servings:** 6

INGREDIENTS
2 cups heavy cream
1 cup milk
3/4 cup sugar
1 Tbs. vanilla extract
4 tablespoons gin
½ cup orange juice
½ lime (peeled and cut up fine)
DIRECTIONS
- NOTE: Freeze your ice cream bowl for at least 24hrs prior to starting!
- Place the milk and cream in a bowl, and mix them together until well combined. Use a whisk to mix in the sugar. Continue to whisk for about 4 minutes until the sugar dissolves. Mix in the vanilla extract. Then whisk in the gin and orange juice and lime.
- Pour the ingredients into your ice cream maker, and let it churn for 25 minutes.
- Serve immediately.

Cucumber Rosemary Honey Rum Sorbet

This one is the adults go-to and you will see why when you try it out. The rosemary gives off a particular flavor mixed in with the cucumber to add a light crispness. But when you add honey to this sorbet, all kinds of flavors start happening to your imagination. We saved the best for last!

Preparation Time About: 2 hours 35 Minutes | **Servings:** 8

INGREDIENTS

4 cups chopped cucumbers
½ cup rosemary
½ cup honey
4 tablespoons rum

DIRECTIONS

- NOTE: Freeze your ice cream bowl for at least 24hrs prior to starting!
- Use a food processor or blender to puree all the ingredients until smooth.
- Pour the ingredients into your ice cream maker, and let it churn for 25-30 minutes.
- Place in an airtight container for up to 2 hours, until desired consistency is reached.

Metric Volume Conversions Chart

US Volume Measure	Metric Equivalent
1/8 teaspoon	0.5 milliliters
1/4 teaspoon	1 milliliter
1/2 teaspoon	2.5 milliliters
3/4 teaspoon	4 milliliters
1 teaspoon	5 milliliters
1 1/4 teaspoons	6 milliliters
1 1/2 teaspoons	7.5 milliliters
1 3/4 teaspoons	8.5 milliliters
2 teaspoons	10 milliliters
1/2 tablespoon	7.5 milliliters
1 tbsp. (3 teaspoons, 1/2 fluid ounce)	15 milliliters
2 tbsp. (1 fluid ounce)	30 milliliters
1/4 cup (4 tablespoons)	60 milliliters
1/3 cup	90 milliliters
1/2 cup (4 fluid ounces)	125 milliliters
2/3 cup	160 milliliters
3/4 cup (6 fluid ounces)	180 milliliters
1 cup (16 tablespoons, 8 fluid ounces)	250 milliliters
1 1/4 cups	300 milliliters
1 1/2 cups (12 fluid ounces)	360 milliliters
1 2/3 cups	400 milliliters
2 cups (1 pint)	500 Milliliters
3 cups	700 Milliliters
4 cups (1 quart)	950 milliliters
1 quart plus 1/4 cup	1 liter
4 quarts (1 gallon)	3.8 liters

Metric Weight Conversion Chart

US Weight Measure	Metric Equivalent
1/2 ounce	7 grams
1/2 ounce	15 grams
3/4 ounce	21 grams
1 ounce	28 grams
1 1/4 ounces	35 grams
1 1/2 ounces	42.5 grams
1 2/3 ounces	45 grams
2 ounces	57 grams
3 ounces	85 grams
4 oz. (1/4 lb.)	113 grams
5 ounces	142 grams
6 ounces	170 grams
7 ounces	198 grams
8 oz. (1/2 lb.)	227 grams
12 oz. (3/4 lb.)	340 Grams

16 oz. (1 lb.)	454 grams
32.5 oz. (2.2 lbs.)	1 kilogram

Temperature Conversion Chart

Degrees Fahrenheit	Degrees Celsius	Cool to Hot
200° F	100° C	Very cool oven
250° F	120° C	Very cool oven
275° F	140° C	Cool oven
300° F	150° C	Cool oven
325° F	160° C	Very moderate oven
350° F	180° C	Moderate oven
375° F	190° C	Moderate oven
400° F	200° C	Moderately hot oven
425° F	220° C	Hot oven
450° F	230° C	Hot oven
475° F	246° C	Very hot oven

CPSIA information can be obtained
at www.ICGtesting.com
Printed in the USA
LVHW060504261020
669798LV00009B/420